The Appeals Court Decision In The Case Of Cariou v. Prince, et al., In Which Twenty Five Of Richard Prince's Canal Zone Paintings Were Found To Be Non-Infringing Of Patrick Cariou's Copyrighted Photographs, And In Which The US District Court Was Ordered To Re-Consider Five Other Of Said Canal Zone Paintings And To Determine Whether Richard Prince Is Entitled To A Fair Use Defense For His Use Of Patrick Cariou's Photographs Therein, Plus The Appendix, Published By The Appeals Court, Delineating In Detail The Use Of Cariou's Photographs By Prince In The Making Of The Canal Zone Paintings On A Painting-By-Painting Basis.

Edited And Annotated For Convenient Reference
By Greg Allen
25 April 2013

11-1197-cv
Patrick Cariou v. Richard Prince, et al.

UNITED STATES COURT OF APPEALS
FOR THE SECOND CIRCUIT

August Term, 2011

(Argued: May 21, 2012 Decided: April 25, 2013)

Docket No. 11-1197-cv

PATRICK CARIOU,

Plaintiff-Appellee,

v.

RICHARD PRINCE,

Defendant-Appellant,

GAGOSIAN GALLERY, INC., LAWRENCE GAGOSIAN,

Defendants-Cross-Defendants-Appellants.

Before: B.D. PARKER, HALL, and WALLACE,* *Circuit Judges.*

Appeal from a judgment of the United States District Court for the Southern District of New York (Batts, *J.*), on Plaintiff-Appellee Patrick Cariou's claim that Defendant-Appellant Richard Prince's artworks infringe on Cariou's registered copyrights in certain photographs. We conclude that the district court applied the incorrect standard to determine whether Prince's artworks make fair use of Cariou's copyrighted photographs. We further conclude that all but five of Prince's works do make fair use of Cariou's copyrighted photographs. With regard to the remaining five Prince artworks, we remand to the district court to consider, in the first instance, whether Prince is entitled to a fair use defense.

REVERSED in part, VACATED in part, and REMANDED.

B.D. PARKER, *J.*, delivered the opinion of the Court, in which HALL, *J.*, joined. WALLACE, *J.*, filed an opinion concurring in part and dissenting in part.

---

* The Honorable J. Clifford Wallace, United States Circuit Judge of the United States Court of Appeals for the Ninth Circuit, sitting by designation.

JOSHUA I. SCHILLER (Jonathan D. Schiller, George F. Carpinello, *on the brief*), Boies, Schiller & Flexner LLP, New York, NY, *for Defendant-Appellant Richard Prince.*

HOLLIS ANNE GONERKA BART, CHAYA WEINBERG-BRODT, DARA G. HAMMERMAN, AZMINA N. JASANI, Withers Bergman LLP, New York, NY, *for Defendants-Appellants Gagosian Gallery, Inc.* and *Lawrence Gagosian.*

DANIEL J. BROOKS (Seth E. Spitzer, Eric A. Boden, *on the brief*), Schnader Harrison Segal & Lewis LLP, New York, NY, *for Plaintiff-Appellee Patrick Cariou.*

ANTHONY T. FALZONE, JULIE A. AHRENS, DANIEL K. NAZER, Stanford Law School Center for Internet and Society, Stanford, CA; VIRGINIA RUTLEDGE, New York, NY; ZACHARY J. ALINDER, JOHN A. POLITO, Bingham McCutchen LLP, San Francisco, CA, *for Amicus The Andy Warhol Foundation for the Visual Arts.*

JOSEPH C. GRATZ, Durie Tangri, LLP, San Francisco, CA; OLIVER METZGER, Google Inc., Mountain View, CA, *for Amicus Google Inc.*

CLIFFORD M. SLOAN, BRADLEY A. KLEIN, Skadden, Arps, Slate, Meagher & Flom LLP, Washington, DC, *for Amici The Association of Art Museum Directors, The Art Institute of Chicago, The Indianapolis Museum of Art, The Metropolitan Museum of Art, The Museum of Modern Art, Museum Associates d.b.a. Los Angeles County Museum of Art, The New Museum, The Solomon R. Guggenheim Foundation, The Walker Art Center,* and *The Whitney Museum of American Art.*

MICHAEL WILLIAMS, DALE M. CENDALI, CLAUDIA RAY, Kirkland & Ellis LLP, Washington, DC, *for*

Amici American Society of Media Photographers, Inc., and *Picture Archive Council of America.*

BARRINGTON D. PARKER, *Circuit Judge*:

In 2000, Patrick Cariou published *Yes Rasta*, a book of classical portraits and landscape photographs that he took over the course of six years spent living among Rastafarians in Jamaica. Richard Prince altered and incorporated several of Cariou's *Yes Rasta* photographs into a series of paintings and collages, called *Canal Zone*, that he exhibited in 2007 and 2008, first at the Eden Rock hotel in Saint Barthélemy ("St. Barth's") and later at New York's Gagosian Gallery.[1] In addition, Gagosian published and sold an exhibition catalog that contained reproductions of Prince's paintings and images from Prince's workshop.

Cariou sued Prince and Gagosian, alleging that Prince's *Canal Zone* works and exhibition catalog infringed on Cariou's copyrights in the incorporated *Yes Rasta* photographs. The defendants raised a fair use defense. After the parties cross-moved for summary judgment, the United States District Court for the Southern District of New York (Batts, *J.*) granted Cariou's motion, denied the defendants', and entered a permanent injunction. It compelled the defendants to deliver to Cariou all infringing works that had not yet been sold, for him to destroy, sell, or otherwise dispose of.

Prince and Gagosian principally contend on appeal that Prince's work is transformative and constitutes fair use of Cariou's copyrighted photographs, and that the district court imposed an incorrect legal standard when it concluded that, in order to qualify for a fair use defense,

---

[1] We refer to Gagosian Gallery and its owner Lawrence Gagosian collectively as "Gagosian" or the "Gallery."

Prince's work must "comment on Cariou, on Cariou's Photos, or on aspects of popular culture closely associated with Cariou or the Photos." *Cariou v. Prince*, 784 F. Supp. 2d 337, 349 (S.D.N.Y. 2011). We agree with Appellants that the law does not require that a secondary use comment on the original artist or work, or popular culture, and we conclude that twenty-five of Prince's artworks do make fair use Cariou's copyrighted photographs. With regard to the remaining five artworks, we remand to the district court, applying the proper standard, to consider in the first instance whether Prince is entitled to a fair use defense.[2]

BACKGROUND

The relevant facts, drawn primarily from the parties' submissions in connection with their cross-motions for summary judgment, are undisputed. Cariou is a professional photographer who, over the course of six years in the mid-1990s, lived and worked among Rastafarians in Jamaica. The relationships that Cariou developed with them allowed him to take a series of portraits and landscape photographs that Cariou published in 2000 in a book titled *Yes Rasta*. As Cariou testified, *Yes Rasta* is "extreme classical photography [and] portraiture," and he did not "want that book to look pop culture at all." Cariou Dep. 187:8-15, Jan. 12, 2010.

Cariou's publisher, PowerHouse Books, Inc., printed 7,000 copies of *Yes Rasta*, in a single printing. Like many, if not most, such works, the book enjoyed limited commercial success. The book is currently out of print. As of January 2010, PowerHouse had sold 5,791 copies, over sixty percent of which sold below the suggested retail price of sixty dollars. PowerHouse has paid Cariou, who holds the copyrights to the *Yes Rasta* photographs, just over

---

[2] The district court's opinion indicated that there are twenty-nine artworks at issue in this case. *See Cariou*, 784 F. Supp. 2d at 344 nn.5, 6. There are actually thirty.

$8,000 from sales of the book. Except for a handful of private sales to personal acquaintances, he has never sold or licensed the individual photographs.

Prince is a well-known appropriation artist. The Tate Gallery has defined appropriation art as "the more or less direct taking over into a work of art a real object or even an existing work of art." J.A. 446. Prince's work, going back to the mid-1970s, has involved taking photographs and other images that others have produced and incorporating them into paintings and collages that he then presents, in a different context, as his own. He is a leading exponent of this genre and his work has been displayed in museums around the world, including New York's Solomon R. Guggenheim Museum and Whitney Museum, San Francisco's Museum of Modern Art, Rotterdam's Museum Boijmans van Beuningen, and Basel's Museum fur Gegenwartskunst. As Prince has described his work, he "completely tr[ies] to change [another artist's work] into something that's completely different." Prince Dep. 338:4-8, Oct. 6, 2009.

Prince first came across a copy of *Yes Rasta* in a bookstore in St. Barth's in 2005. Between December 2007 and February 2008, Prince had a show at the Eden Rock hotel in St. Barth's that included a collage, titled *Canal Zone (2007)*, comprising 35 photographs torn out of *Yes Rasta* and pinned to a piece of plywood. Prince altered those photographs significantly, by among other things painting "lozenges" over their subjects' facial features and using only portions of some of the images. In June 2008, Prince purchased three additional copies of *Yes Rasta*. He went on to create thirty additional artworks in the *Canal Zone* series, twenty-nine of which incorporated partial or whole images from *Yes Rasta*.[3] The portions of *Yes Rasta*

[3] Images of the Prince artworks, along with the *Yes Rasta* photographs incorporated therein, appear in the Appendix to this opinion. The Appendix is available at http://www.ca2.uscourts.gov/11-1197apx.htm.

photographs used, and the amount of each artwork that they constitute, vary significantly from piece to piece. In certain works, such as *James Brown Disco Ball*, Prince affixed headshots from *Yes Rasta* onto other appropriated images, all of which Prince placed on a canvas that he had painted. In these, Cariou's work is almost entirely obscured. The Prince artworks also incorporate photographs that have been enlarged or tinted, and incorporate photographs appropriated from artists other than Cariou as well. *Yes Rasta* is a book of photographs measuring approximately 9.5" x 12". Prince's artworks, in contrast, comprise inkjet printing and acrylic paint, as well as pasted-on elements, and are several times that size. For instance, *Graduation* measures 72 3/4" x 52 1/2" and *James Brown Disco Ball* 100 1/2" x 104 1/2". The smallest of the Prince artworks measures 40" x 30", or approximately ten times as large as each page of *Yes Rasta*.

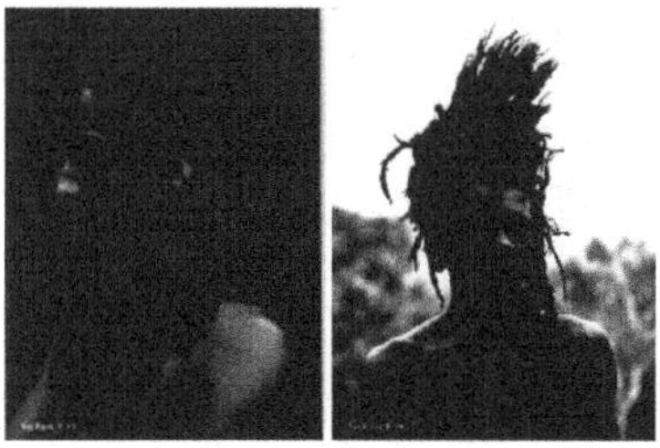

Patrick Cariou, Photographs from *Yes Rasta*, pp. 11, 59

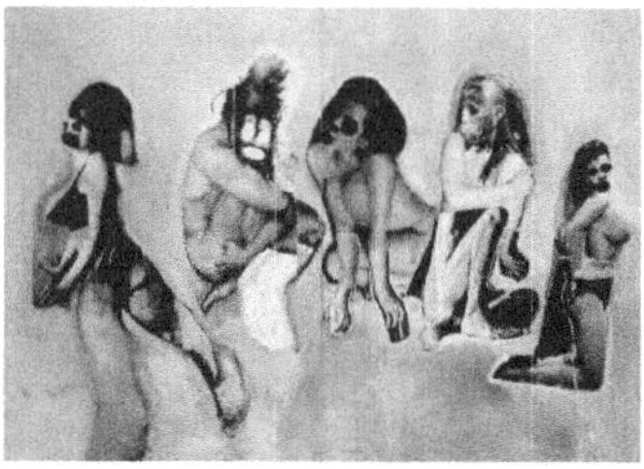

Richard Prince, *James Brown Disco Ball*

In other works, such as *Graduation*, Cariou's original work is readily apparent: Prince did little more than paint blue lozenges over the subject's eyes and mouth, and paste a picture of a guitar over the subject's body.

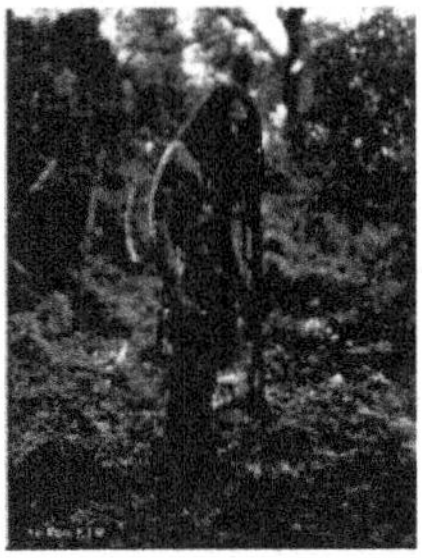

Patrick Cariou, Photograph from *Yes Rasta*, p. 118

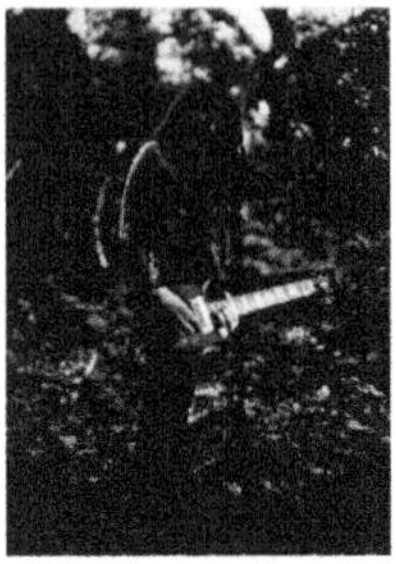

Richard Prince, *Graduation*

Between November 8 and December 20, 2008, the Gallery put on a show featuring twenty-two of Prince's *Canal Zone* artworks, and also published and sold an exhibition catalog from the show. The catalog included all of the *Canal Zone* artworks (including those not in the Gagosian show) except for one, as well as, among other things, photographs showing *Yes Rasta* photographs in Prince's studio. Prince never sought or received permission from Cariou to use his photographs.

Prior to the Gagosian show, in late August, 2008, a gallery owner named Cristiane Celle contacted Cariou and asked if he would be interested in discussing the possibility of an exhibit in New York City. Celle did not mention *Yes Rasta*, but did express interest in photographs Cariou took of surfers, which he published in 1998 in the aptly titled *Surfers*. Cariou responded that *Surfers* would be republished in 2008, and inquired whether Celle might also be interested in a book Cariou had recently completed on gypsies. The two subsequently met and discussed Cariou's exhibiting work in Celle's gallery, including prints from *Yes Rasta*. They did not select a date or photographs to exhibit, nor did they finalize any other details about the possible future show.

At some point during the *Canal Zone* show at Gagosian, Celle learned that Cariou's photographs were "in the show with Richard Prince." Celle then phoned Cariou and, when he did not respond, Celle mistakenly concluded that he was "doing something with Richard Prince . . . . [Maybe] he's not pursuing me because he's doing something better, bigger with this person. . . . [H]e didn't want to tell the French girl I'm not doing it with you, you know, because we had started a relation and that would have been bad." Celle Dep. 88:15-89:7, Jan. 26, 2010. At that point, Celle decided that she would not put on a "Rasta show" because it had been "done already," and that any future Cariou exhibition she put on would be of photographs from *Surfers*. Celle remained interested in exhibiting prints from *Surfers*, but Cariou never followed through.

According to Cariou, he learned about the Gagosian *Canal Zone* show from Celle in December 2008. On December 30, 2008, he sued Prince, the Gagosian Gallery, and Lawrence Gagosian, raising claims of copyright infringement. *See* 17 U.S.C. §§ 106, 501. The defendants asserted a fair use defense, arguing that Prince's artworks are transformative of Cariou's photographs and, accordingly, do not violate Cariou's copyrights. *See, e.g., Campbell v. Acuff-Rose Music, Inc.*, 510 U.S. 569, 578-79 (1994). Ruling on the parties' subsequently-filed cross-motions for summary judgment, the district court (Batts, *J.*) "impose[d] a requirement that the new work in some way comment on, relate to the historical context of, or critically refer back to the original works" in order to be qualify as fair use, and stated that "Prince's Paintings are transformative only to the extent that they comment on the Photos." *Cariou v. Prince*, 784 F. Supp. 2d 337, 348-49 (S.D.N.Y. 2011). The court concluded that "Prince did not intend to comment on Cariou, on Cariou's Photos, or on aspects of popular culture closely associated with Cariou or the Photos when he appropriated the Photos," *id.* at 349, and for that reason rejected the defendants' fair use defense and granted summary judgment to Cariou. The district court also granted sweeping injunctive relief, ordering the defendants to "deliver up for impounding, destruction, or other disposition, as [Cariou] determines, all infringing copies of the Photographs, including the Paintings and unsold copies of the *Canal Zone* exhibition book, in their possession." *Id.* at 355.[4] This appeal followed.

DISCUSSION

I.

We review a grant of summary judgment *de novo*. *See Blanch v. Koons*, 467 F.3d 244, 249-50 (2d Cir. 2006). The well known standards for summary judgment set forth in Rule 56(c) apply. *See* Fed. R. Civ. P. 56. "Although fair use is a mixed question of law and fact, this court has on numerous occasions resolved fair use determinations at the summary judgment stage where . . . there are no genuine issues of material fact." *Blanch*, 467 F.3d at 250 (quotation marks and brackets omitted); *see also Harper & Row, Publishers, Inc. v. Nation Enters.*, 471 U.S. 539, 560 (1985); *Castle Rock Entm't, Inc. v. Carol Publ'g Grp., Inc.*, 150 F.3d 132, 137 (2d Cir. 1998). This case lends itself to that approach.

II.

The purpose of the copyright law is "[t]o promote the Progress of Science and useful Arts . . . ." U.S. Const., Art. I, § 8, cl. 8. As Judge Pierre Leval of this court has explained, "[t]he copyright is not an inevitable, divine, or natural right that confers on authors the absolute ownership of their creations. It is designed rather to stimulate activity and progress in the arts for

[4] At oral argument, counsel for Cariou indicated that he opposes the destruction of any of the works of art that are the subject of this litigation.

the intellectual enrichment of the public." Pierre N. Leval, *Toward a Fair Use Standard*, 103 Harv. L. Rev. 1105, 1107 (1990) (hereinafter "Leval"). Fair use is "necessary to fulfill [that] very purpose." *Campbell*, 510 U.S. at 575. Because "'excessively broad protection would stifle, rather than advance, the law's objective,'" fair use doctrine "mediates between" "the property rights [copyright law] establishes in creative works, which must be protected up to a point, and the ability of authors, artists, and the rest of us to express them- or ourselves by reference to the works of others, which must be protected up to a point." *Blanch*, 467 F.3d at 250 (brackets omitted) (quoting Leval at 1109).

The doctrine was codified in the Copyright Act of 1976, which lists four non-exclusive factors that must be considered in determining fair use. Under the statute,

> [T]he fair use of a copyrighted work . . . for purposes such as criticism, comment, news reporting, teaching (including multiple copies for classroom use), scholarship, or research, is not an infringement of copyright. In determining whether the use made of a work in any particular case is a fair use the factors to be considered shall include –
>
> (1) the purpose and character of the use, including whether such use is of a commercial nature or is for nonprofit educational purposes;
>
> (2) the nature of the copyrighted work;
>
> (3) the amount and substantiality of the portion used in relation to the copyrighted work as a whole; and
>
> (4) the effect of the use upon the potential market for the value of the copyrighted work.

17 U.S.C. § 107. As the statute indicates, and as the Supreme Court and our court have recognized, the fair use determination is an open-ended and context-sensitive inquiry. *Campbell*, 510 U.S. at 577-78; *Blanch*, 467 F.3d at 251. The statute "employs the terms 'including' and

'such as' in the preamble paragraph to indicate the illustrative and not limitative function of the examples given, which thus provide only general guidance about the sorts of copying that courts and Congress most commonly had found to be fair uses." *Campbell*, 510 U.S. at 577-78 (quotation marks and citation omitted). The "ultimate test of fair use . . . is whether the copyright law's goal of 'promoting the Progress of Science and useful Arts' . . . would be better served by allowing the use than by preventing it." *Castle Rock*, 150 F.3d at 141 (brackets and citation omitted).

The first statutory factor to consider, which addresses the manner in which the copied work is used, is "[t]he heart of the fair use inquiry." *Blanch*, 467 F.3d at 251. We ask

> whether the new work merely 'supersedes the objects' of the original creation, or instead adds something new, with a further purpose or different character, altering the first with new expression, meaning, or message[,] . . . in other words, whether and to what extent the new work is transformative. . . . [T]ransformative works . . . lie at the heart of the fair use doctrine's guarantee of breathing space . . . .

Campbell, 510 U.S. at 579 (citations and some quotation marks omitted) (quoting *Folsom v. Marsh*, 9 F. Cas. 342, 348 *No. 4,901) (C.C.D. Mass. 1841) (Story, *J.*)). "If 'the secondary use adds value to the original – if [the original work] is used as raw material, transformed in the creation of new information, new aesthetics, new insights and understandings – this is the very type of activity that the fair use doctrine intends to protect for the enrichment of society.'" *Castle Rock*, 150 F.3d at 142 (quoting Leval 1111). For a use to be fair, it "must be productive and must employ the quoted matter in a different manner or for a different purpose from the original." Leval at 1111.

The district court imposed a requirement that, to qualify for a fair use defense, a secondary use must "comment on, relate to the historical context of, or critically refer back to the original works." *Cariou*, 784 F. Supp. 2d at 348. Certainly, many types of fair use, such as satire and parody, invariably comment on an original work and/or on popular culture. For example, the rap group 2 Live Crew's parody of Roy Orbison's "Oh, Pretty Woman" "was clearly intended to ridicule the white-bread original." *Campbell*, 510 U.S. at 582 (quotation marks omitted). Much of Andy Warhol's work, including work incorporating appropriated images of Campbell's soup cans or of Marilyn Monroe, comments on consumer culture and explores the relationship between celebrity culture and advertising. As even Cariou concedes, however, the district court's legal premise was not correct. The law imposes no requirement that a work comment on the original or its author in order to be considered transformative, and a secondary work may constitute a fair use even if it serves some purpose other than those (criticism, comment, news reporting, teaching, scholarship, and research) identified in the preamble to the statute. *Id.* at 577; *Harper & Row*, 471 U.S. at 561. Instead, as the Supreme Court as well as decisions from our court have emphasized, to qualify as a fair use, a new work generally must alter the original with "new expression, meaning, or message." *Campbell*, 510 U.S. at 579; *see also Blanch*, 467 F.3d at 253 (original must be employed "in the creation of new information, new aesthetics, new insights and understandings" (quotation marks omitted)); *Castle Rock*, 150 F.3d at 142.

Here, our observation of Prince's artworks themselves convinces us of the transformative nature of all but five, which we discuss separately below. These twenty-five of Prince's artworks manifest an entirely different aesthetic from Cariou's photographs. Where Cariou's serene and deliberately composed portraits and landscape photographs depict the natural beauty of Rastafarians and their surrounding environs, Prince's crude and jarring works, on the other hand, are hectic and provocative. Cariou's black-and-white photographs were printed in a 9 1/2" x 12" book. Prince has created collages on canvas that incorporate color, feature distorted human and other forms and settings, and measure between ten and nearly a hundred times the size of the photographs. Prince's composition, presentation, scale, color palette, and media are fundamentally different and new compared to the photographs, as is the expressive nature of Prince's work. *See Campbell*, 510 U.S. at 579.

Prince's deposition testimony further demonstrates his drastically different approach and aesthetic from Cariou's. Prince testified that he "[doesn't] have any really interest in what [another artist's] original intent is because . . . what I do is I completely try to change it into something that's completely different. . . . I'm trying to make a kind of fantastic, absolutely hip, up to date, contemporary take on the music scene." Prince Dep. 338:4-339:3, Oct. 6, 2009. As the district court determined, Prince's *Canal Zone* artworks relate to a "post-apocalyptic screenplay" Prince had planned, and "emphasize themes [of Prince's planned screenplay] of equality of the sexes; highlight 'the three relationships in the world, which are men and women, men and men, and women and women'; and portray a contemporary take on the music scene." *Cariou*, 784 F. Supp. 2d at 349; *see* Prince Dep. 339:3-7, Oct. 6, 2009.

The district court based its conclusion that Prince's work is not transformative in large part on Prince's deposition testimony that he "do[es]n't really have a message," that he was not "trying to create anything with a new meaning or a new message," and that he "do[es]n't have any . . . interest in [Cariou's] original intent." *Cariou*, 784 F. Supp. 2d at 349; *see* Prince Dep. 45:25-46:2, 338:5-6, 360:18-20, Oct. 6, 2009. On appeal, Cariou argues that we must hold Prince to his testimony and that we are not to consider how Prince's works may reasonably be perceived unless Prince claims that they were satire or parody. No such rule exists, and we do not analyze satire or parody differently from any other transformative use.

It is not surprising that, when transformative use is at issue, the alleged infringer would go to great lengths to explain and defend his use as transformative. Prince did not do so here. However, the fact that Prince did not provide those sorts of explanations in his deposition – which might have lent strong support to his defense – is not dispositive. What is critical is how the work in question appears to the reasonable observer, not simply what an artist might say about a particular piece or body of work. Prince's work could be transformative even without commenting on Cariou's work or on culture, and even without Prince's stated intention to do so. Rather than confining our inquiry to Prince's explanations of his artworks, we instead examine how the artworks may "reasonably be perceived" in order to assess their transformative nature. *Campbell*, 510 U.S. at 582; *Leibovitz v. Paramount Pictures Corp.*, 137 F.3d 109, 113-14 (2d Cir. 1998) (evaluating parodic nature of advertisement in light of how it "may reasonably be perceived"). The focus of our infringement analysis is primarily on the Prince artworks themselves, and we see twenty-five of them as transformative as a matter of law.

In this respect, the Seventh Circuit's recent decision in *Brownmark Films, LLC v. Comedy Partners*, 682 F.3d 687 (7th Cir. 2012), is instructive. There, the court rejected the appellant's argument that copyright infringement claims cannot be disposed of at the motion-to-dismiss stage, and affirmed the district court's dismissal of such a claim under Fed. R. Civ. P. 12(b)(6). *Brownmark Films*, 682 F.3d at 690. Considering whether an episode of the animated television show *South Park* presented a parody (and therefore a protected fair use) of a viral internet video titled "What What (In The Butt)," the court concluded that "[w]hen the two works . . . are viewed side-by-side, the *South Park* episode is clearly a parody of the original . . . video." *Id.* at 692. For that reason, "the only two pieces of evidence needed to decide the question of fair use in [*Brownmark* were] the original version of [the video] and the episode at issue." *Id.* at 690.

Here, looking at the artworks and the photographs side-by-side, we conclude that Prince's images, except for those we discuss separately below, have a different character, give Cariou's photographs a new expression, and employ new aesthetics with creative and communicative results distinct from Cariou's. Our conclusion should not be taken to suggest, however, that any cosmetic changes to the photographs would necessarily constitute fair use. A secondary work may modify the original without being transformative. For instance, a derivative work that merely presents the same material but in a new form, such as a book of synopses of televisions shows, is not transformative. *See Castle Rock*, 150 F.3d at 143; *Twin Peaks Prods., Inc. v. Publ'ns Int'l, Ltd.*, 996 F.2d 1366, 1378 (2d Cir. 1993). In twenty-five of his artworks, Prince has not presented the same material as Cariou in a different manner, but instead has "add[ed] something new" and presented images with a fundamentally different aesthetic. *Leibovitz*, 137 F.3d at 114.

The first fair use factor – the purpose and character of the use – also requires that we consider whether the allegedly infringing work has a commercial or nonprofit educational purpose. *See, e.g., Blanch*, 467 F.3d at 253. That being said, "nearly all of the illustrative uses listed in the preamble paragraph of § 107, including news reporting, comment, criticism, teaching, scholarship, and research . . . are generally conducted for profit." *Campbell*, 510 U.S. at 584 (quotation marks omitted). "The commercial/nonprofit dichotomy concerns the unfairness that arises when a secondary user makes unauthorized use of copyrighted material to capture significant revenues as a direct consequence of copying the original work." *Am. Geophysical Union v. Texaco Inc.*, 60 F.3d 913, 922 (2d Cir. 1994). This factor must be applied with caution because, as the Supreme Court has recognized, Congress "could not have intended" a rule that commercial uses are presumptively unfair. *Campbell*, 510 U.S. at 584 Instead, "[t]he more transformative the new work, the less will be the significance of other factors, like commercialism, that may weigh against a finding of fair use." *Id.* at 579. Although there is no question that Prince's artworks are commercial, we do not place much significance on that fact due to the transformative nature of the work.

We turn next to the fourth statutory factor, the effect of the secondary use upon the potential market for the value of the copyrighted work, because such discussion further demonstrates the significant differences between Prince's work, generally, and Cariou's. Much of the district court's conclusion that Prince and Gagosian infringed on Cariou's copyrights was apparently driven by the fact that Celle decided not to host a *Yes Rasta* show at her gallery once she learned of the Gagosian *Canal Zone* show. The district court determined that this factor weighs against Prince because he "has unfairly damaged both the actual and potential markets for Cariou's original work and the potential market for derivative use licenses for Cariou's original work." *Cariou*, 784 F. Supp. 2d at 353.

Contrary to the district court's conclusion, the application of this factor does not focus principally on the question of damage to Cariou's derivative market. We have made clear that "our concern is not whether the secondary use suppresses or even destroys the market for the original work or its potential derivatives, but whether the secondary use *usurps* the market of the original work." *Blanch*, 467 F.3d at 258 (quotation marks omitted) (emphasis added); *NXIVM Corp. v. Ross Inst.*, 364 F.3d 471, 481-82 (2d Cir. 2004). "The market for potential derivative uses includes only those that creators of original works would in general develop or license others to develop." *Campbell*, 510 U.S. at 592. Our court has concluded that an accused infringer has usurped the market for copyrighted works, including the derivative market, where the infringer's target audience and the nature of the infringing content is the same as the original. For instance, a book of trivia about the television show *Seinfeld* usurped the show's market because the trivia book "substitute[d] for a derivative market that a television program copyright owner . . . would in general develop or license others to develop." *Castle Rock*, 150 F.3d at 145 (quotation marks omitted). Conducting this analysis, we are mindful that "[t]he more transformative the secondary use, the less likelihood that the secondary use substitutes for the original," even though "the fair use, being transformative, might well harm, or even destroy, the market for the original." *Id.*

As discussed above, Celle did not decide against putting on a *Yes Rasta* show because it had already been done at Gagosian, but rather because she mistakenly believed that Cariou had collaborated with Prince on the Gagosian show. Although certain of Prince's artworks contain significant portions of certain of Cariou's photographs, neither Prince nor the *Canal Zone* show usurped the market for those photographs. Prince's audience is very different from Cariou's, and there is no evidence that Prince's work ever touched – much less usurped – either the primary or derivative market for Cariou's work. There is nothing in the record to suggest that Cariou would ever develop or license secondary uses of his work in the vein of Prince's artworks. Nor does anything in the record suggest that Prince's artworks had any impact on the marketing of the photographs. Indeed, Cariou has not aggressively marketed his work, and has earned just over $8,000 in royalties from *Yes Rasta* since its publication. He has sold four prints from the book, and only to personal acquaintances.

Prince's work appeals to an entirely different sort of collector than Cariou's. Certain of the *Canal Zone* artworks have sold for two million or more dollars. The invitation list for a dinner that Gagosian hosted in conjunction with the opening of the *Canal Zone* show included a number of the wealthy and famous such as the musicians Jay-Z and Beyonce Knowles, artists Damien Hirst and Jeff Koons, professional football player Tom Brady, model Gisele Bundchen, *Vanity Fair* editor Graydon Carter, *Vogue* editor Anna Wintour, authors Jonathan Franzen and Candace Bushnell, and actors Robert DeNiro, Angelina Jolie, and Brad Pitt. Prince sold eight artworks for a total of $10,480,000, and exchanged seven others for works by painter Larry Rivers and by sculptor Richard Serra. Cariou on the other hand has not actively marketed his work or sold work for significant sums, and nothing in the record suggests that anyone will not now purchase Cariou's work, or derivative non-transformative works (whether Cariou's own or licensed by him) as a result of the market space that Prince's work has taken up. This fair use factor therefore weighs in Prince's favor.

The next statutory factor that we consider, the nature of the copyrighted work, "calls for recognition that some works are closer to the core of intended copyright protection than others, with the consequence that fair use is more difficult to establish when the former works are copied." *Campbell*, 510 U.S. at 586. We consider "'(1) whether the work is expressive or creative, . . . with a greater leeway being allowed to a claim of fair use where the work is factual or informational, and (2) whether the work is published or unpublished, with the scope for fair use involving unpublished works being considerably narrower.'" *Blanch*, 467 F.3d at 256 (quoting 2 Howard B. Abrams, *The Law of Copyright*, § 15:52 (2006)).

Here, there is no dispute that Cariou's work is creative and published. Accordingly, this factor weighs against a fair use determination. However, just as with the commercial character of Prince's work, this factor "may be of limited usefulness where," as here, "the creative work of art is being used for a transformative purpose." *Bill Graham Archives v. Dorling Kindersley Ltd.*, 448 F.3d 605, 612 (2d Cir. 2006).

The final factor that we consider in our fair use inquiry is "the amount and substantiality of the portion used in relation to the copyrighted work as a whole." 17 U.S.C. § 107(3). We ask "whether the quantity and value of the materials used[] are reasonable in relation to the purpose of the copying." *Blanch*, 467 F.3d at 257 (quotation marks omitted). In other words, we consider the proportion of the original work used, and not how much of the secondary work comprises the original.

Many of Prince's works use Cariou's photographs, in particular the portrait of the dreadlocked Rastafarian at page 118 of *Yes Rasta*, the Rastafarian on a burro at pages 83 to 84, and the dreadlocked and bearded Rastafarian at page 108, in whole or substantial part. In some works, such as *Charlie Company*, Prince did not alter the source photograph very much at all. In others, such as *Djuana Barnes, Natalie Barney, Renee Vivien and Romaine Brooks take over the Guanahani*, the entire source photograph is used but is also heavily obscured and altered to the point that Cariou's original is barely recognizable. Although "[n]either our court nor any of our sister circuits has ever ruled that the copying of an entire work *favors* fair use[,] . . . . courts have concluded that such copying does not necessarily weigh against fair use because copying the entirety of a work is sometimes necessary to make a fair use of the image." *Bill Graham*, 448 F.3d at 613. "[T]he third-factor inquiry must take into account that the extent of permissible copying varies with the purpose and character of the use." *Id.* (internal quotation marks omitted).

The district court determined that Prince's "taking was substantially greater than necessary." *Cariou*, 784 F. Supp. 2d at 352. We are not clear as to how the district court could arrive at such a conclusion. In any event, the law does not require that the secondary artist may take no more than is necessary. *See Campbell*, 510 U.S. at 588; *Leibovitz*, 137 F.3d at 114. We consider not only the quantity of the materials taken but also "their quality and importance" to the original work. *Campbell*, 510 U.S. at 587. The secondary use "must be [permitted] to 'conjure up' *at least* enough of the original" to fulfill its transformative purpose. *Id.* at 588 (emphasis added); *Leibovitz*, 137 F.3d at 114. Prince used key portions of certain of Cariou's photographs. In doing that, however, we determine that in twenty-five of his artworks, Prince transformed those photographs into something new and different and, as a result, this factor weighs heavily in Prince's favor.

As indicated above, there are five artworks that, upon our review, present closer questions. Specifically, *Graduation*, *Meditation*, *Canal Zone (2008)*, *Canal Zone (2007)*, and *Charlie Company* do not sufficiently differ from the photographs of Cariou's that they incorporate for us confidently to make a determination about their transformative nature as a matter of law. Although the minimal alterations that Prince made in those instances moved the work in a different direction from Cariou's classical portraiture and landscape photos, we can not say with certainty at this point whether those artworks present a "new expression, meaning, or message." *Campbell*, 510 U.S. at 579.

Certainly, there are key differences in those artworks compared to the photographs they incorporate. *Graduation*, for instance, is tinted blue, and the jungle background is in softer focus than in Cariou's original. Lozenges painted over the subject's eyes and mouth – an alteration that appears frequently throughout the *Canal Zone* artworks – make the subject appear anonymous, rather than as the strong individual who appears in the original. Along with the enlarged hands and electric guitar that Prince pasted onto his canvas, those alterations create the impression that the subject is not quite human. Cariou's photograph, on the other hand, presents a human being in his natural habitat, looking intently ahead. Where the photograph presents someone comfortably at home in nature, *Graduation* combines divergent elements to create a sense of discomfort. However, we cannot say for sure whether *Graduation* constitutes fair use or whether Prince has transformed Cariou's work enough to render it transformative.

We have the same concerns with *Meditation*, *Canal Zone (2007)*, *Canal Zone (2008)*, and *Charlie Company*. Each of those artworks differs from, but is still similar in key aesthetic ways, to Cariou's photographs. In *Meditation*, Prince again added lozenges and a guitar to the same photograph that he incorporated into *Graduation*, this time cutting the subject out of his background, switching the direction he is facing, and taping that image onto a blank canvas. In *Canal Zone (2007)*, Prince created a gridded collage using 31 different photographs of Cariou's, many of them in whole or significant part, with alterations of some of those photographs limited to lozenges or cartoonish appendages painted or drawn on. *Canal Zone (2008)* incorporates six photographs of Cariou's in whole or in part, including the same subject as *Meditation* and *Graduation*. Prince placed the subject, with lozenges and guitar, on a background comprising components of various landscape photographs, taped together. The cumulative effect is of the subject in a habitat replete with lush greenery, not dissimilar from many of Cariou's *Yes Rasta* photographs. And *Charlie Company* prominently displays four copies of Cariou's photograph of a Rastafarian riding a donkey, substantially unaltered, as well as two copies of a seated nude woman with lozenges covering all six faces. Like the other works just discussed, *Charlie Company* is aesthetically similar to Cariou's original work because it maintains the pastoral background and individual focal point of the original photograph – in this case, the man on the burro. While the lozenges, repetition of the images, and addition of the nude female unarguably change the tenor of the piece, it is unclear whether these alterations amount to a sufficient transformation of the original work of art such that the new work is transformative.

We believe the district court is best situated to determine, in the first instance, whether such relatively minimal alterations render *Graduation*, *Meditation*, *Canal Zone (2007)*, *Canal Zone (2008)*, and *Charlie Company* fair uses (including whether the artworks are transformative) or whether any impermissibly infringes on Cariou's copyrights in his original photographs. We remand for that determination.

III.

In addition to its conclusion that Prince is liable for infringing on Cariou's copyrights, the district court determined that the Gagosian defendants are liable as vicarious and contributory infringers. *Cariou*, 784 F. Supp. 2d at 354. With regard to the twenty-five of Prince's artworks, which, as we have held, do not infringe on Cariou's copyrights, neither Lawrence Gagosian nor the Gallery may be liable as a vicarious or contributory infringer. *See Faulkner v. Nat'l Geographic Enters., Inc.*, 409 F.3d 26, 40 (2d Cir. 2005). If the district court concludes on remand that Prince is liable as a direct infringer with regard to any of the remaining five works, the district court should determine whether the Gagosian defendants should be held liable, directly or secondarily, as a consequence of their actions with regard to those works. *See* Copyright Act, 17 U.S.C. §§ 106(1), (2), (3), (5).

CONCLUSION

For the reasons discussed, we hold that all except five (*Graduation*, *Meditation*, *Canal Zone (2007)*, *Canal Zone (2008)*, and *Charlie Company*) of Prince's artworks make fair use of Cariou's photographs. We express no view as to whether the five are also entitled to a fair use defense. We REMAND with respect to those five so that the district court, applying the proper standard, can determine in the first instance whether any of them infringes on Cariou's copyrights or whether Prince is entitled to a fair use defense with regard to those artworks as well. The judgment of the district court is **REVERSED** in part and **VACATED** in part.[5] The case is **REMANDED** for further proceedings consistent with this opinion.

---

[5] Because we reverse the district court with regard to the twenty-five of the artworks, and leave open the question of fair use with regard to the remaining five, we vacate the district court's injunction. In the event that Prince and Gagosian are ultimately held liable for copyright infringement, and in light of all parties' agreement at oral argument that the destruction of Prince's artwork would be improper and against the public interest, a position with which we agree, the district court should revisit what injunctive relief, if any, is appropriate. *See eBay, Inc. v. MercExchange, L.L.C.*, 547 U.S. 388, 391 (2006); *Salinger v. Colting*, 607 F.3d 68, 77 (2d Cir. 2010).

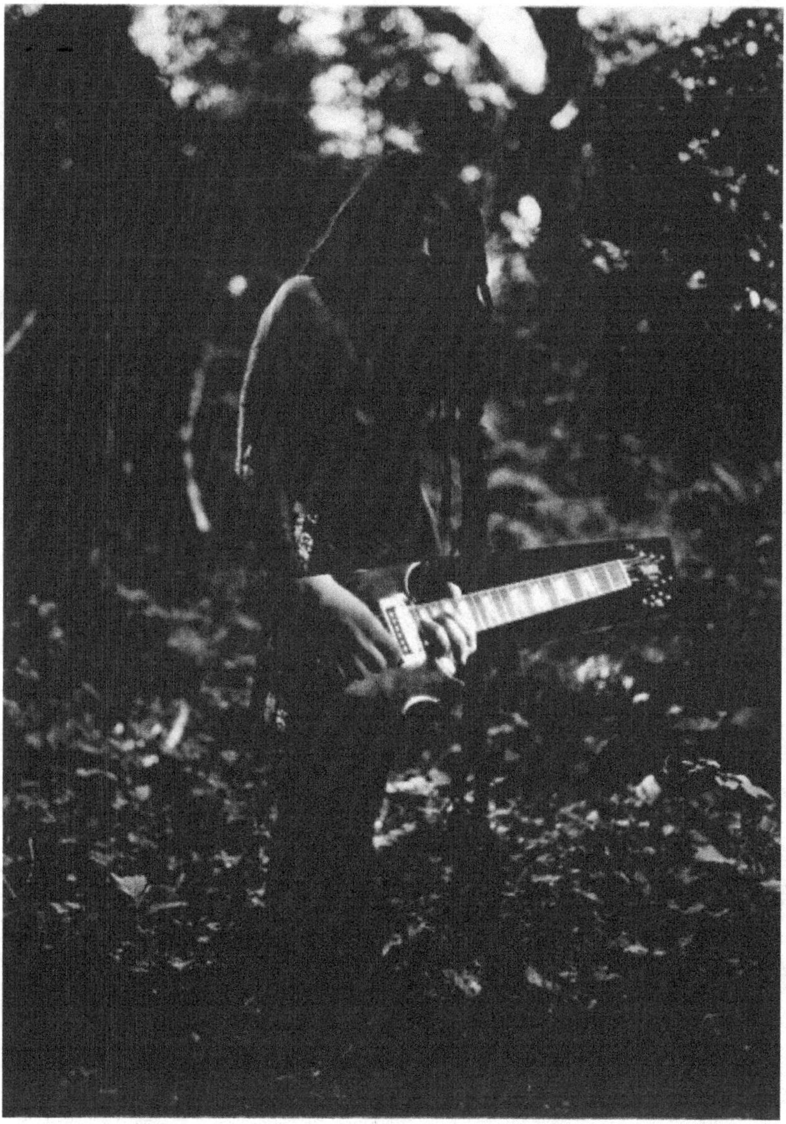

A

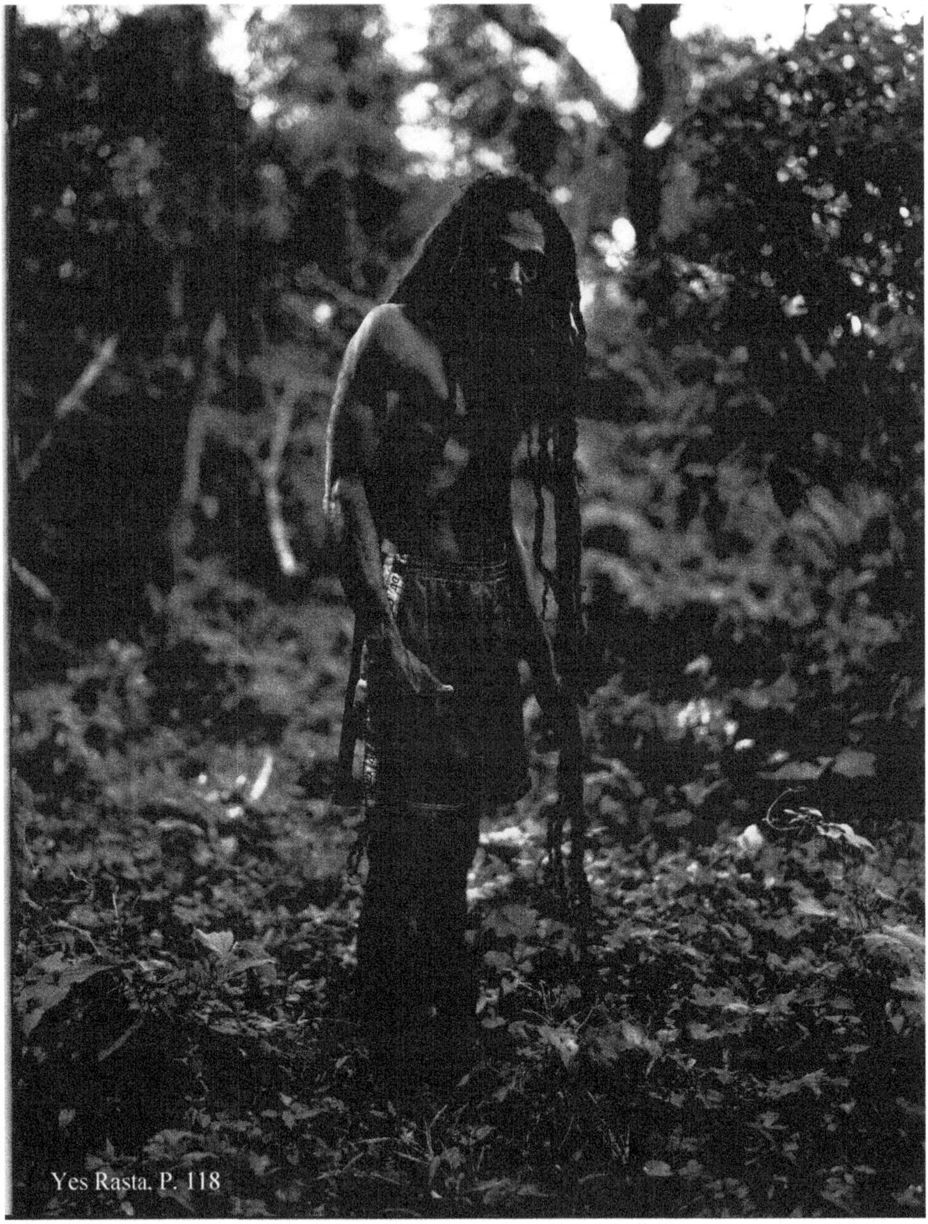
Yes Rasta. P. 118

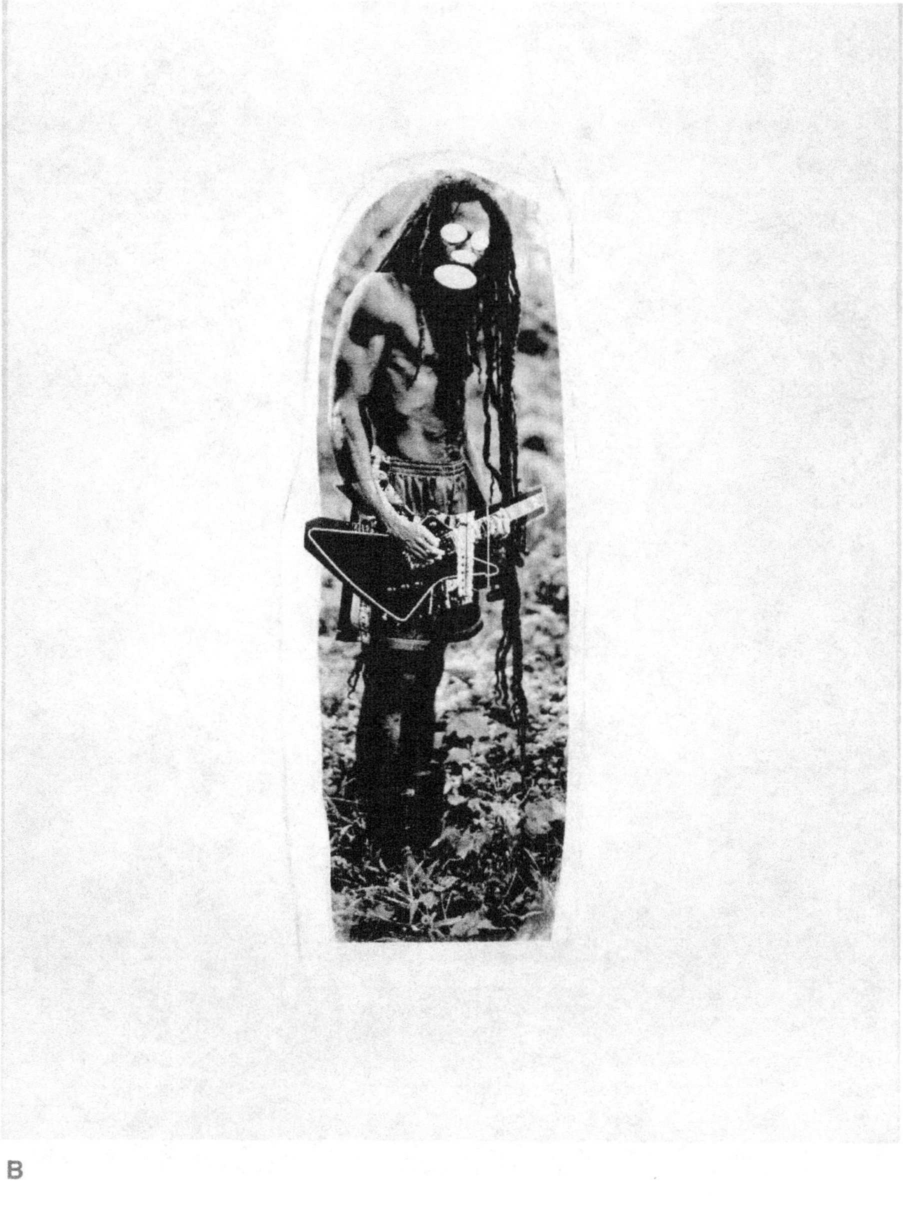

B

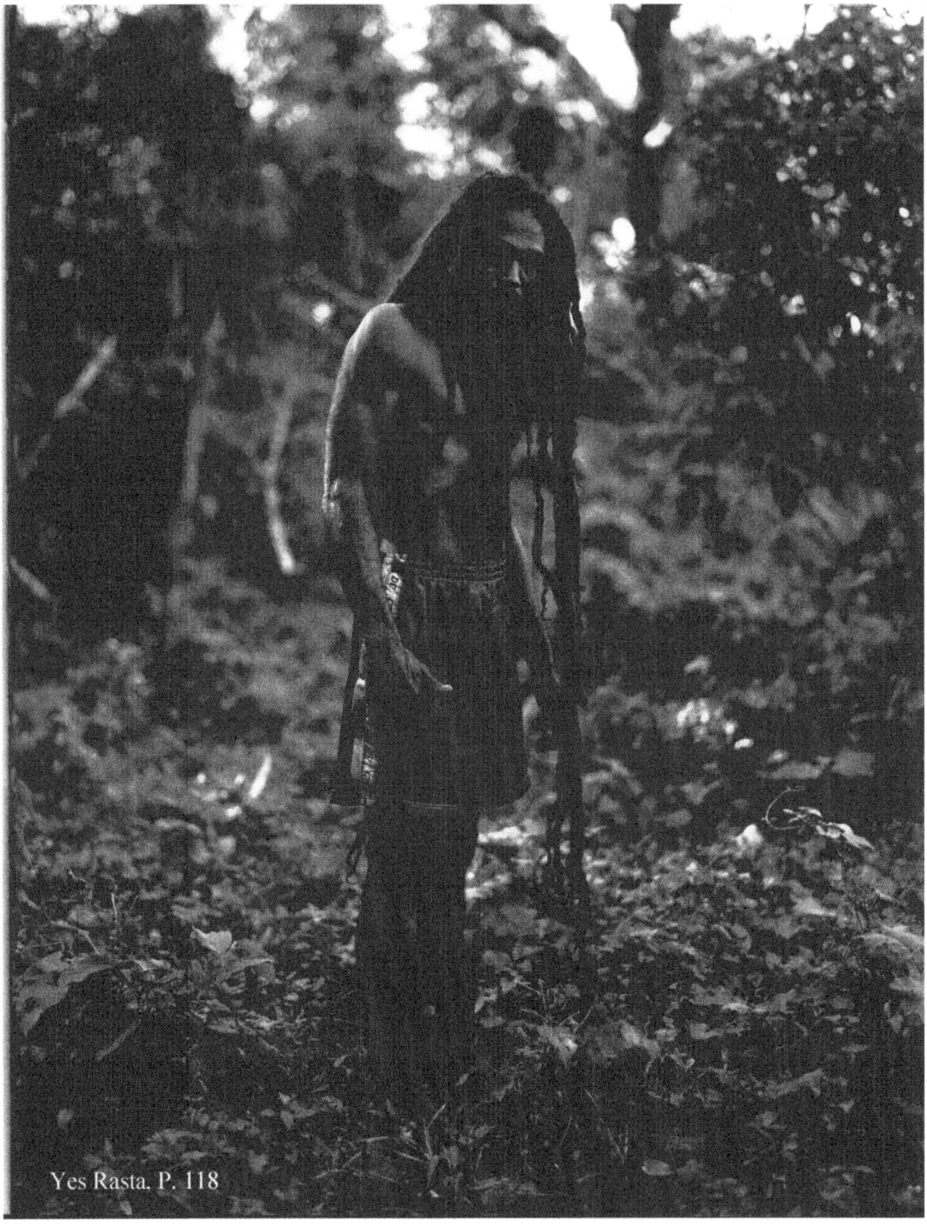

Yes Rasta. P. 118

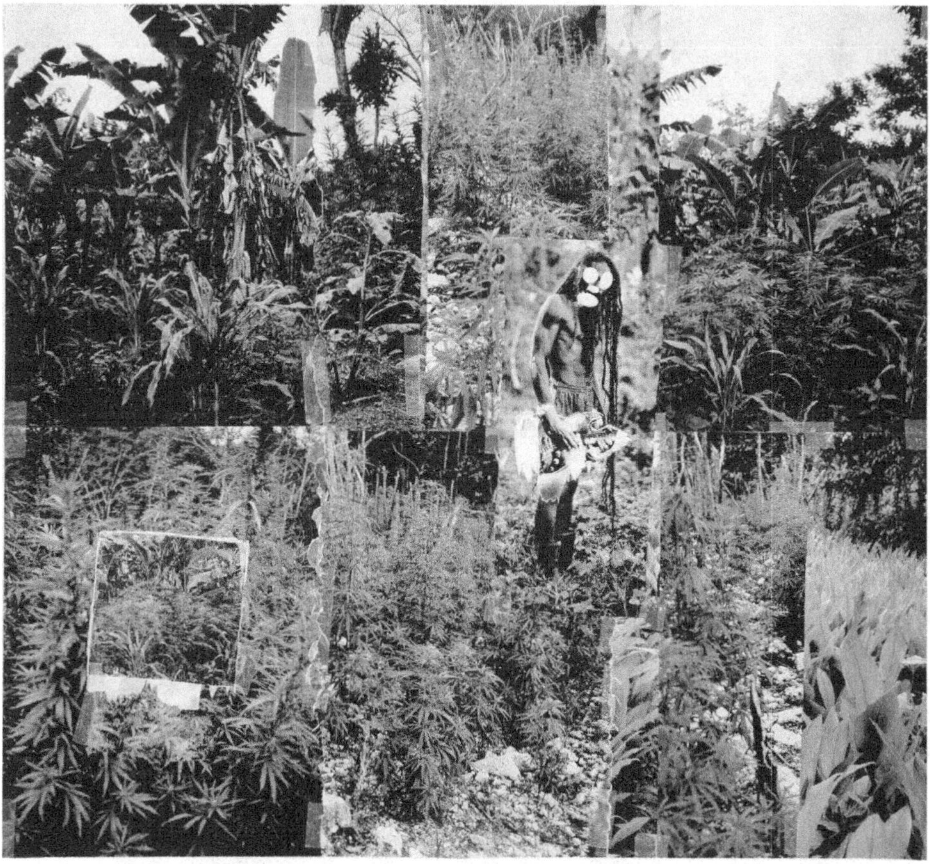

C

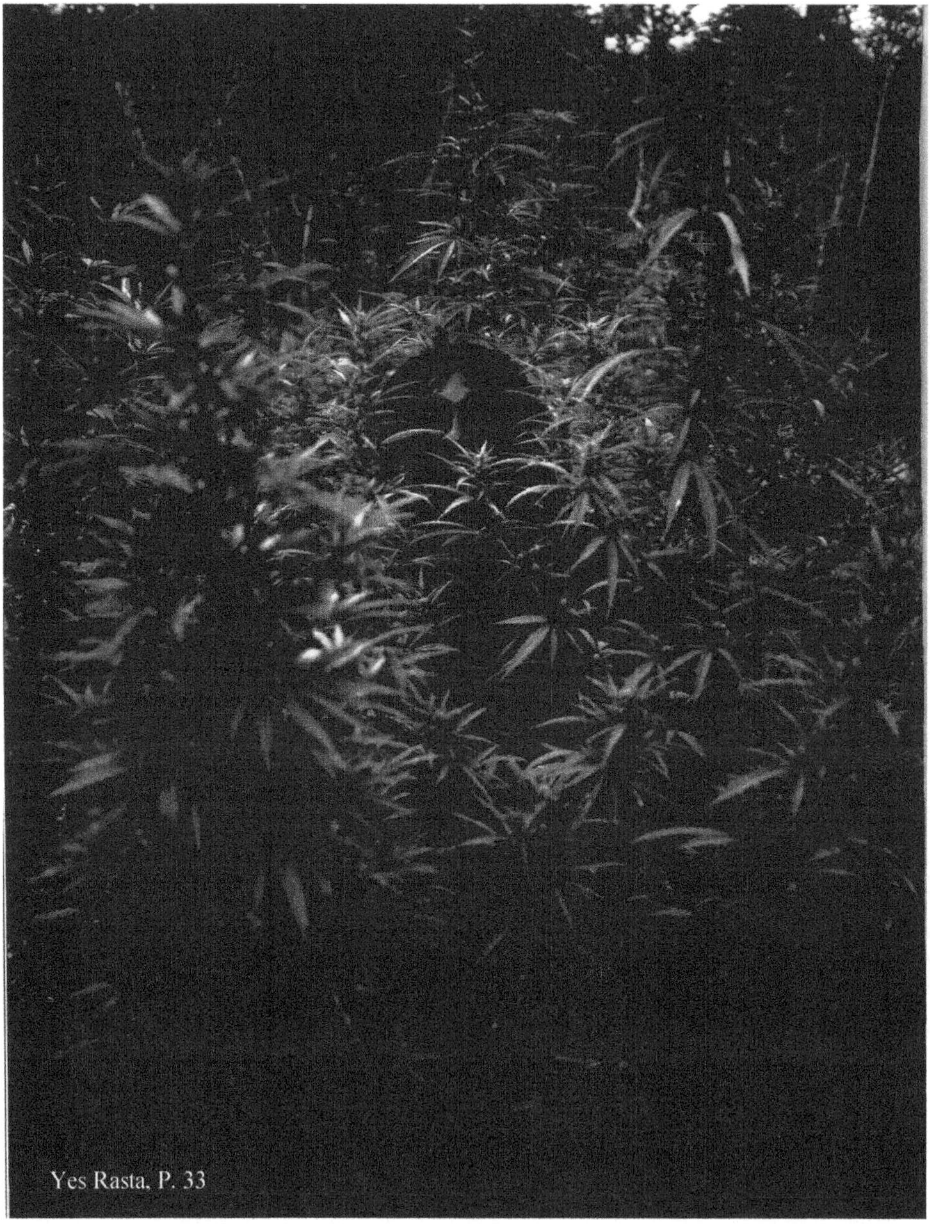

Yes Rasta, P. 33

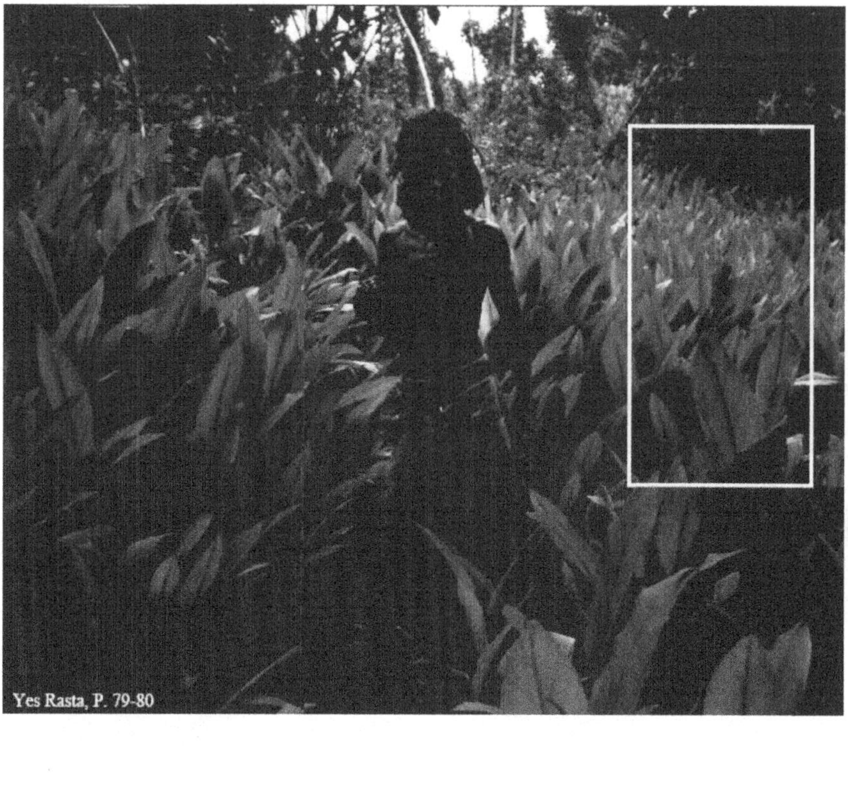
Yes Rasta, P. 79-80

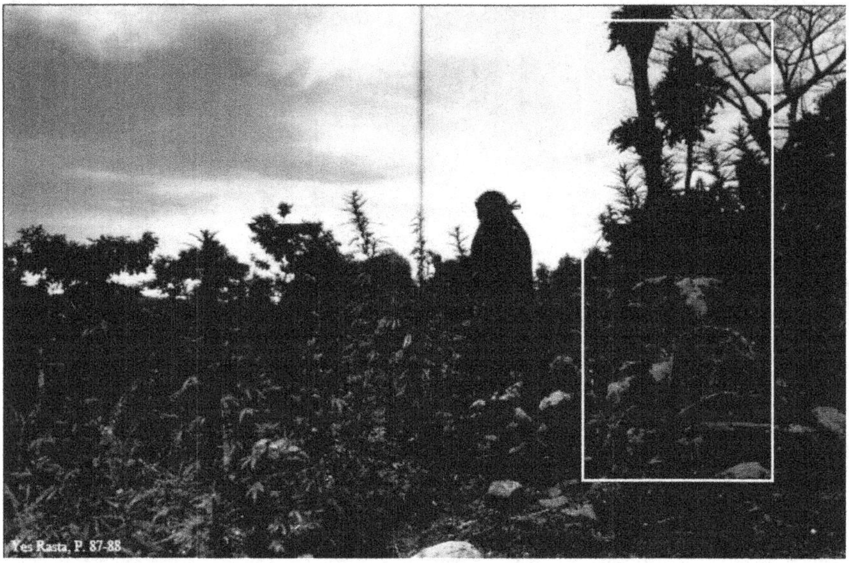
Yes Rasta, P. 87-88

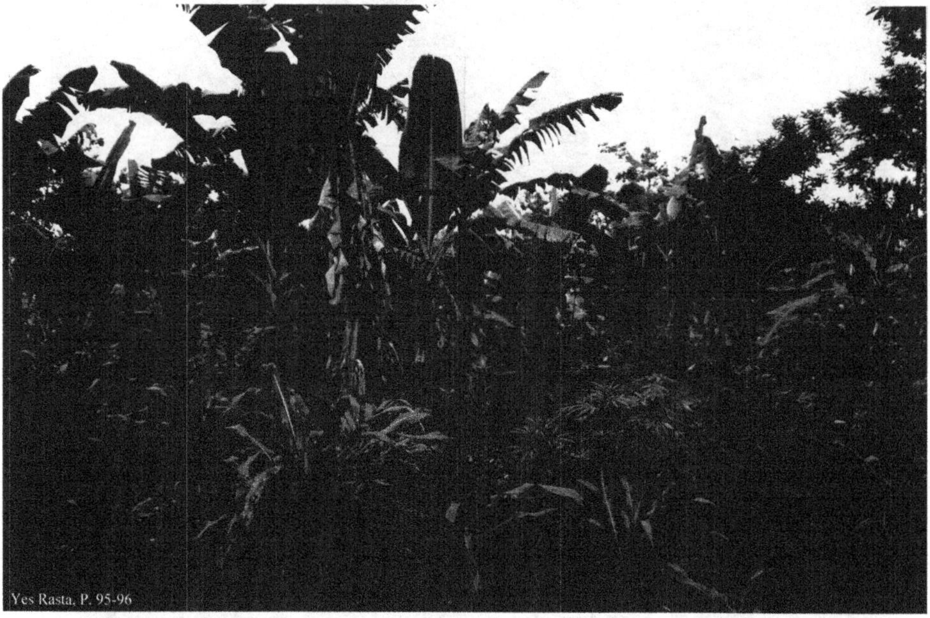

Yes Rasta, P. 95-96

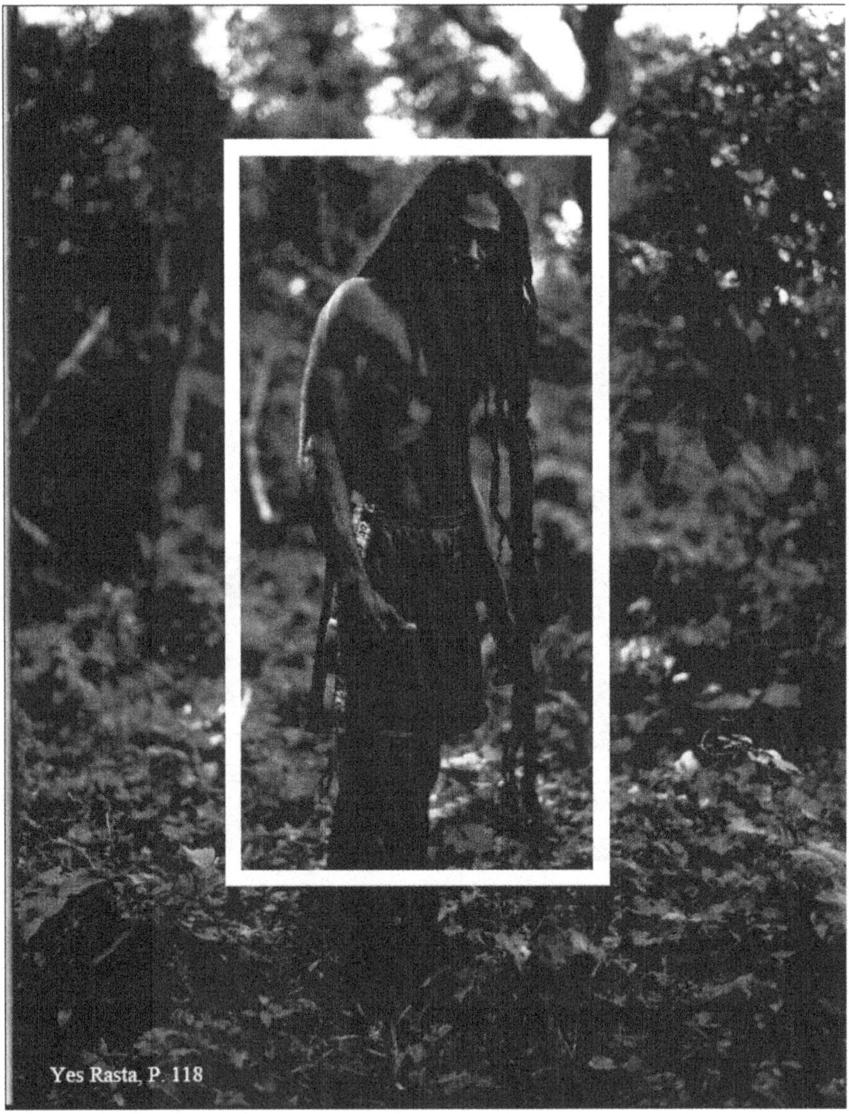
Yes Rasta, P. 118

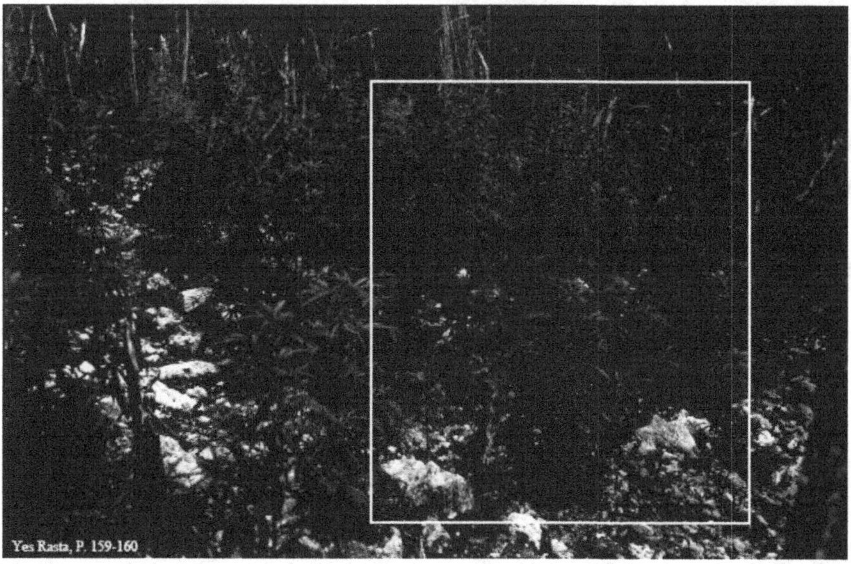

Yes Rasta, P. 159-160

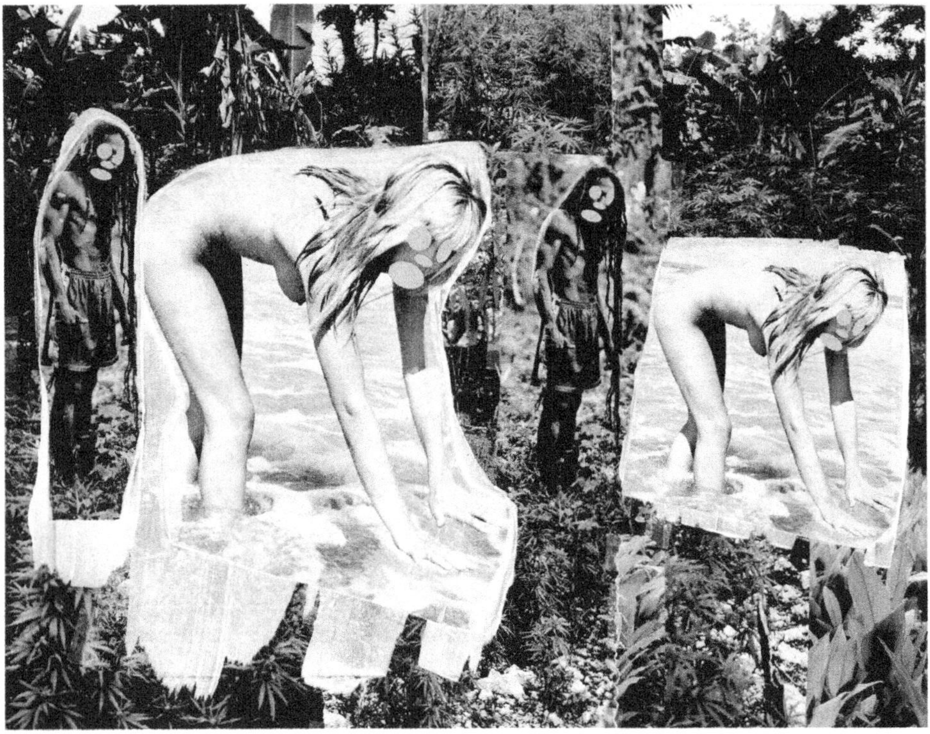

D

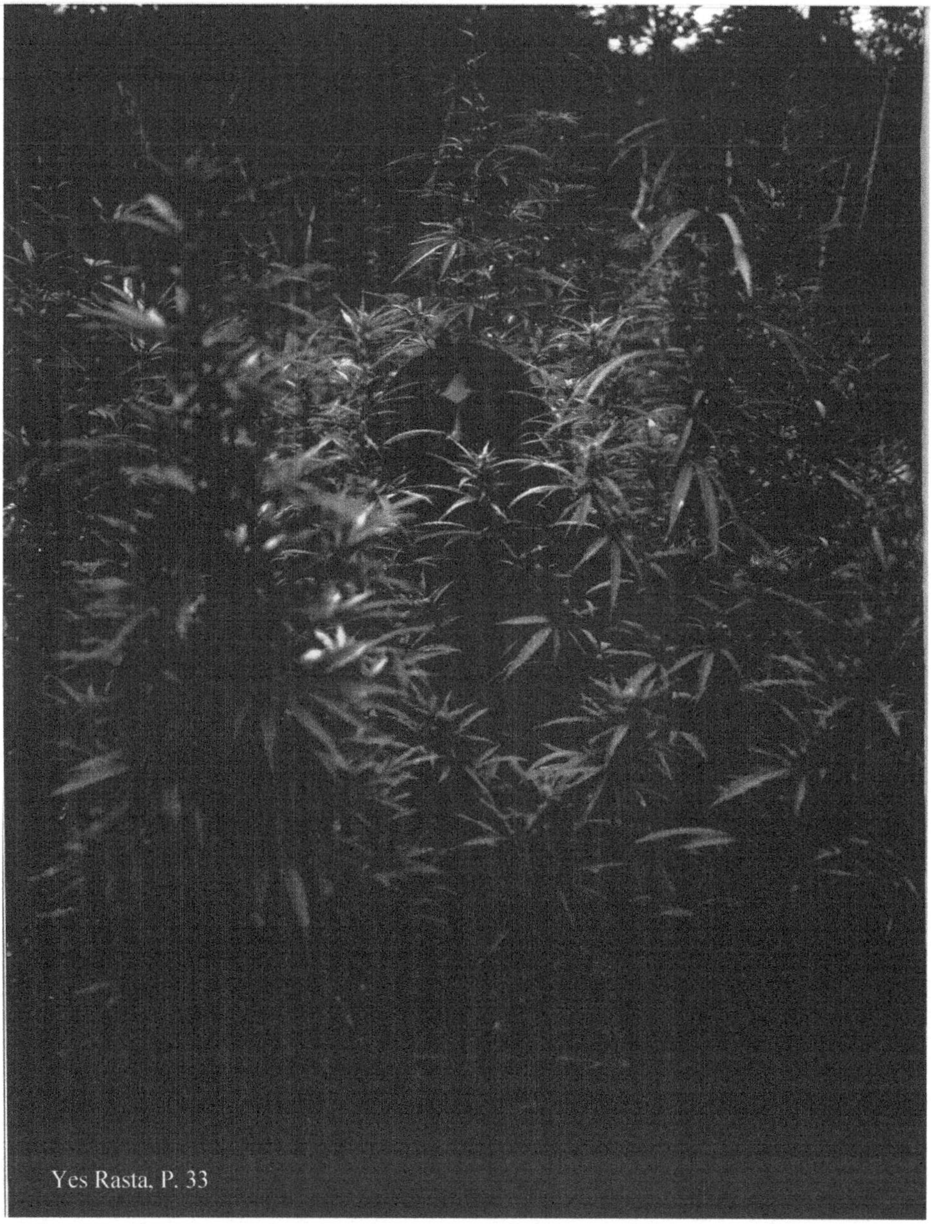
Yes Rasta, P. 33

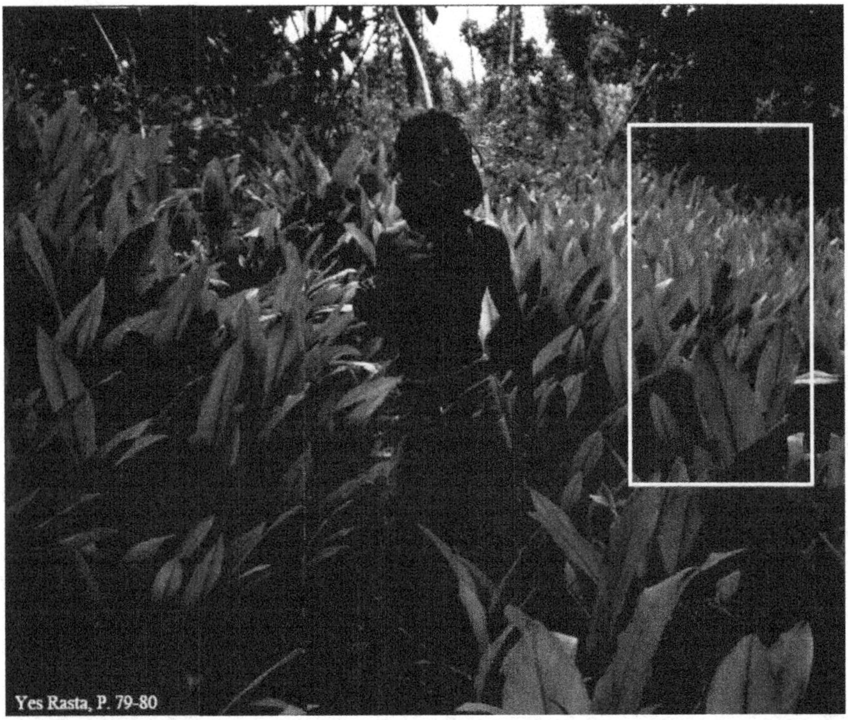
Yes Rasta, P. 79-80

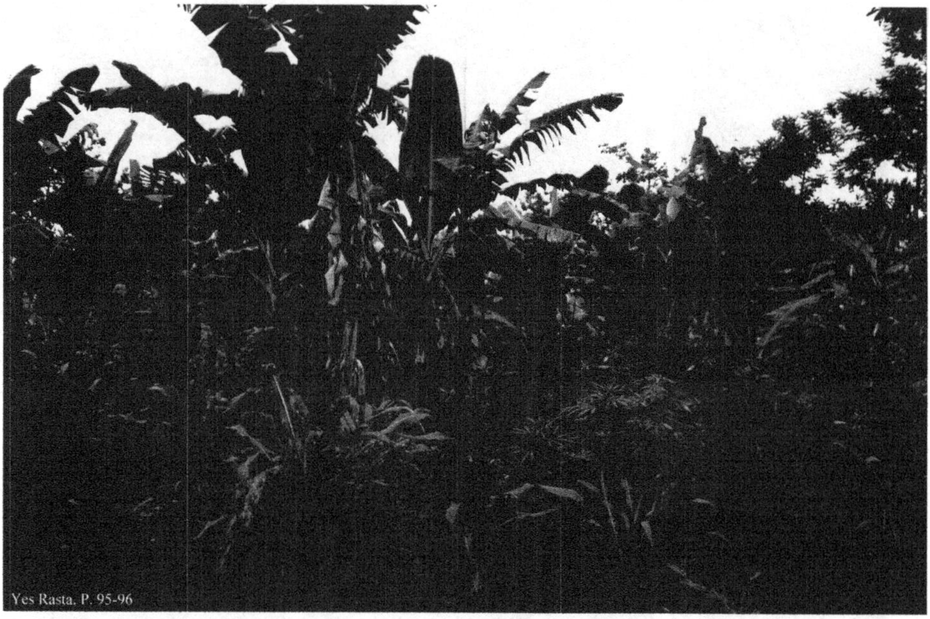

Yes Rasta, P. 95-96

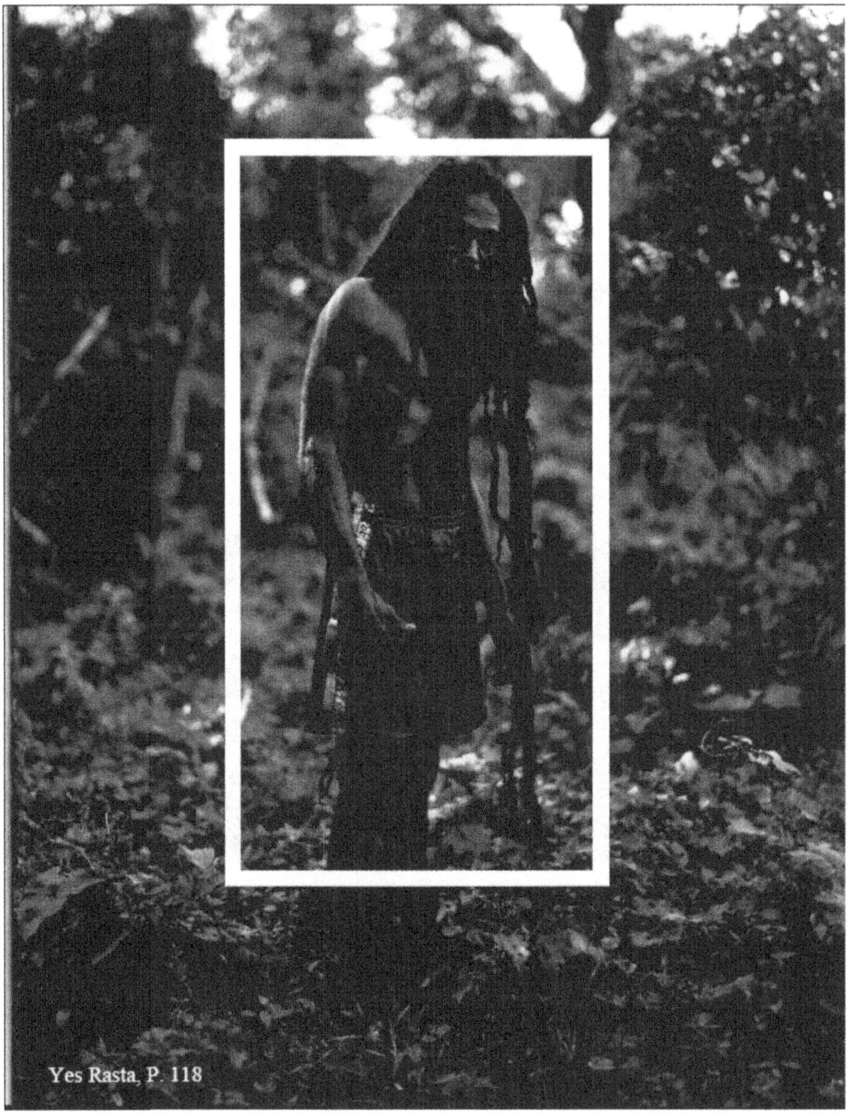

Yes Rasta, P. 118

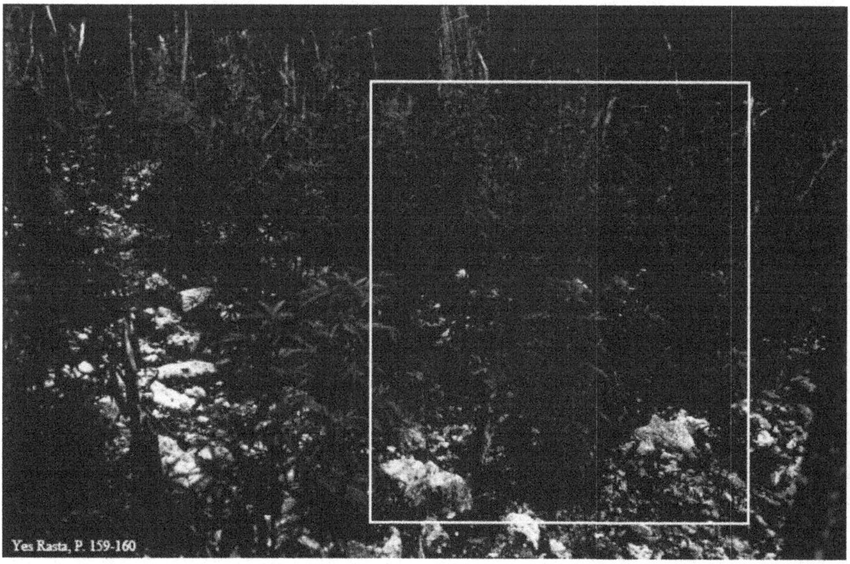
Yes Rasta, P. 159-160

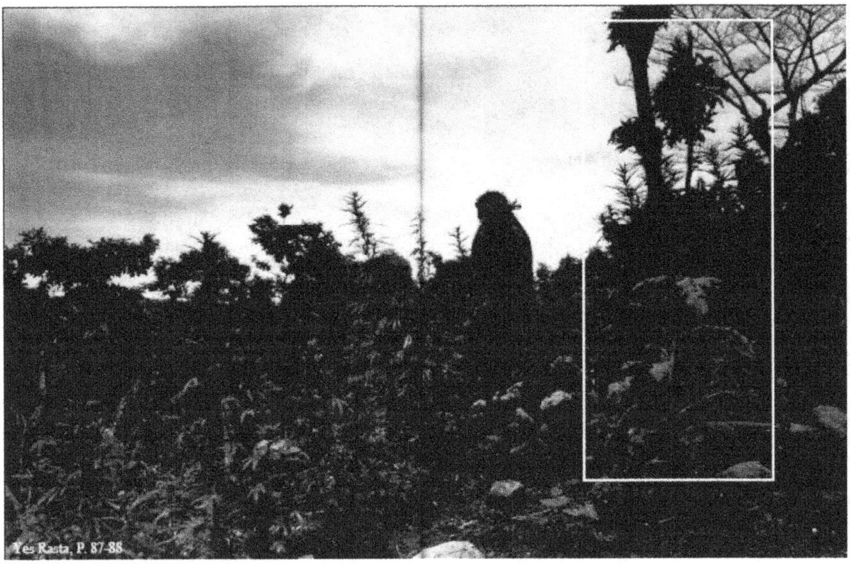
Yes Rasta, P. 87-88

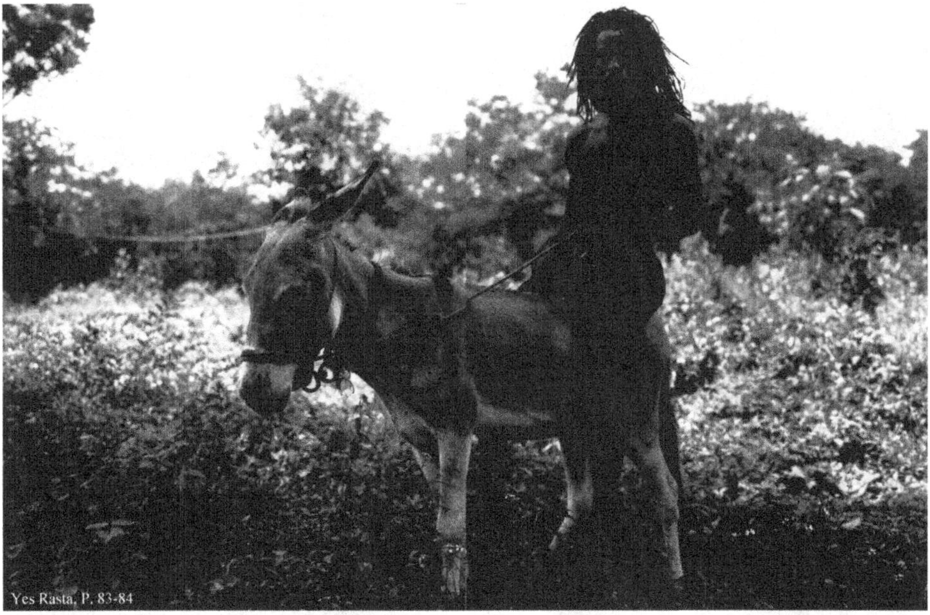

Yes Rasta, P. 83-84

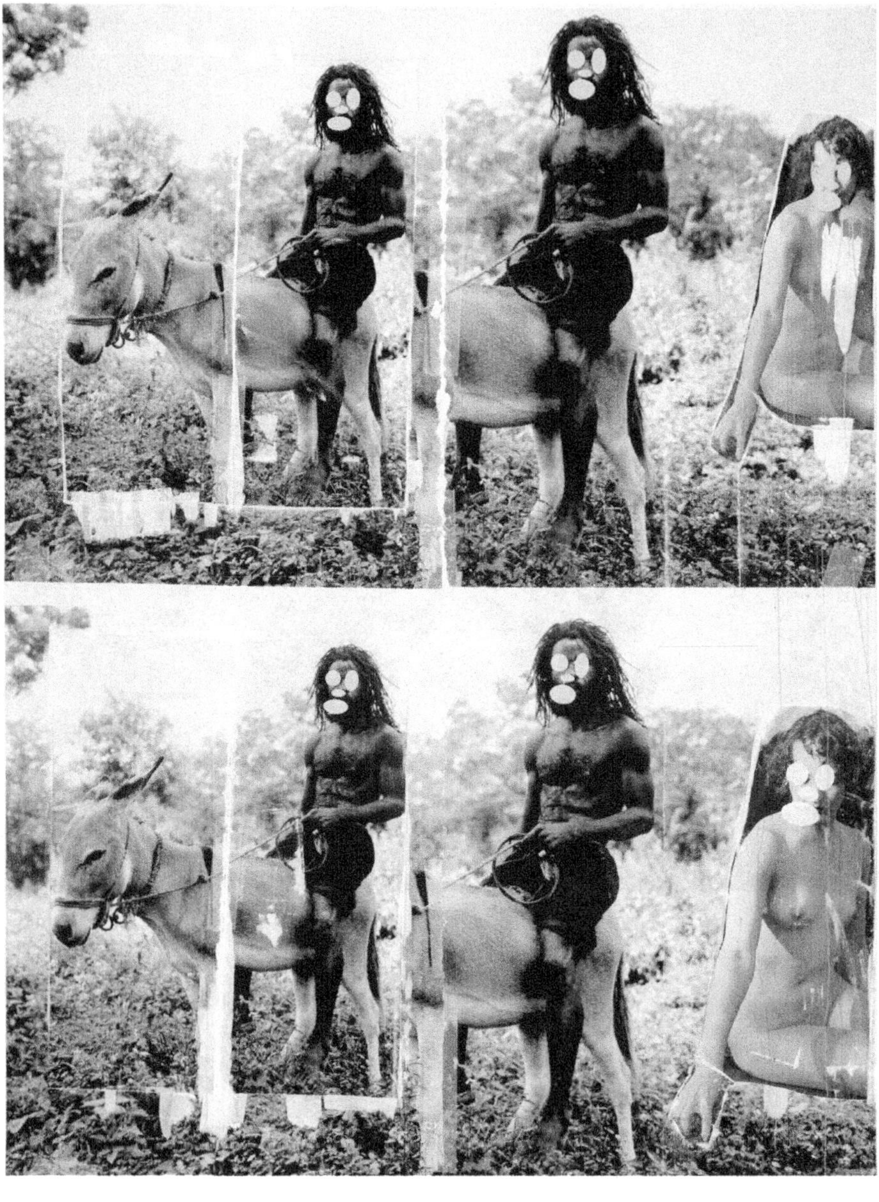

E

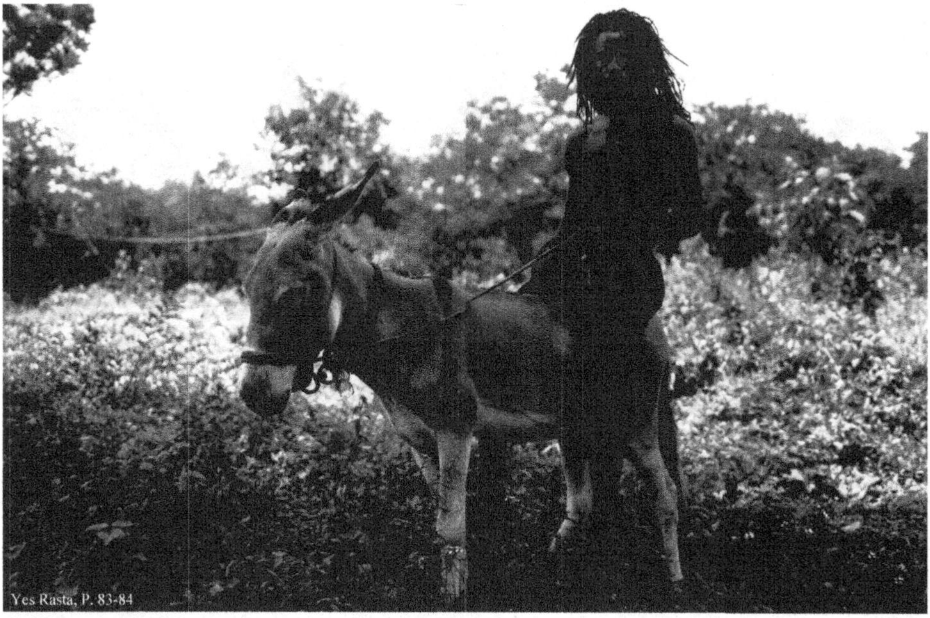
Yes Rasta, P. 83-84

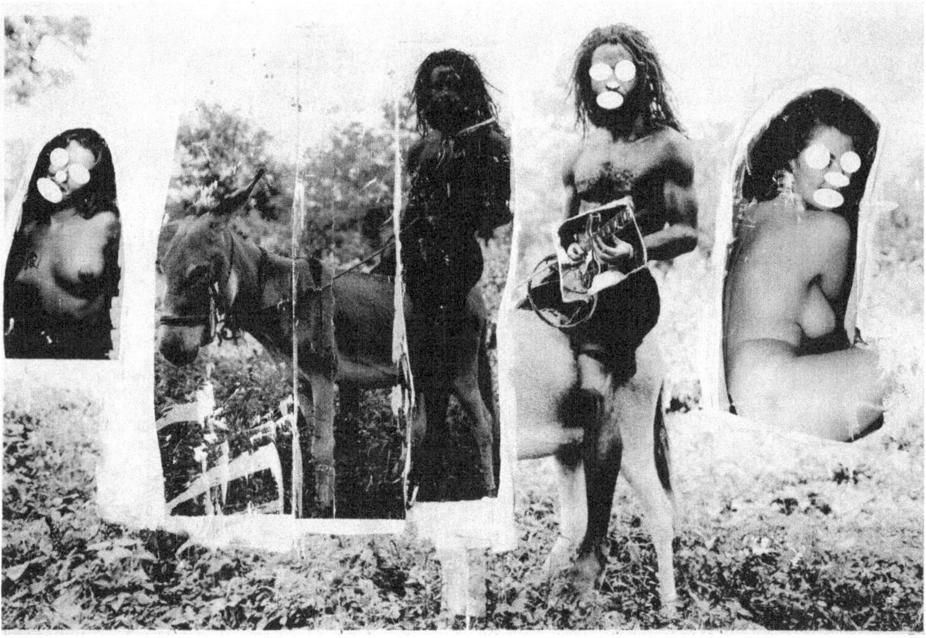

F

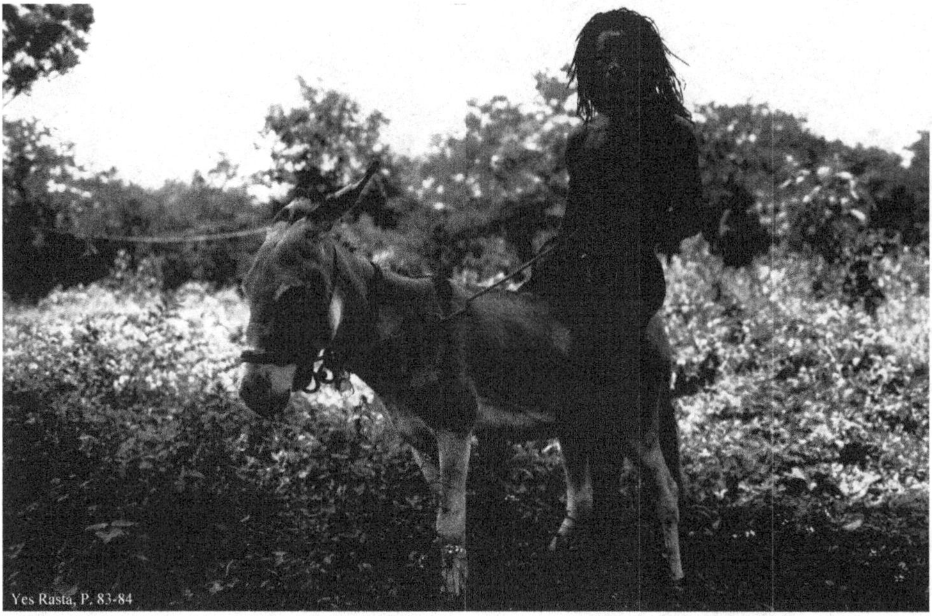

Yes Rasta, P. 83-84

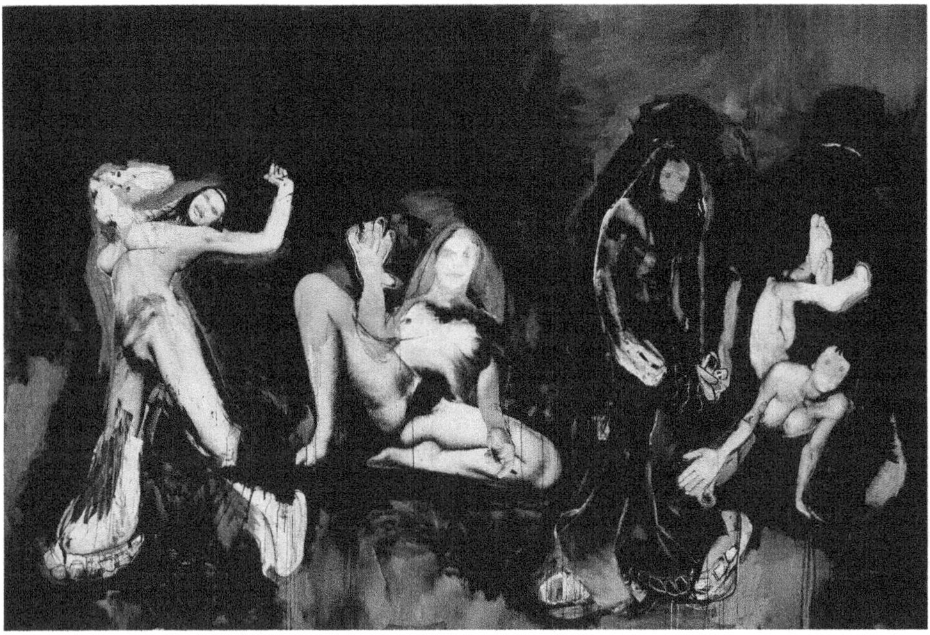

G

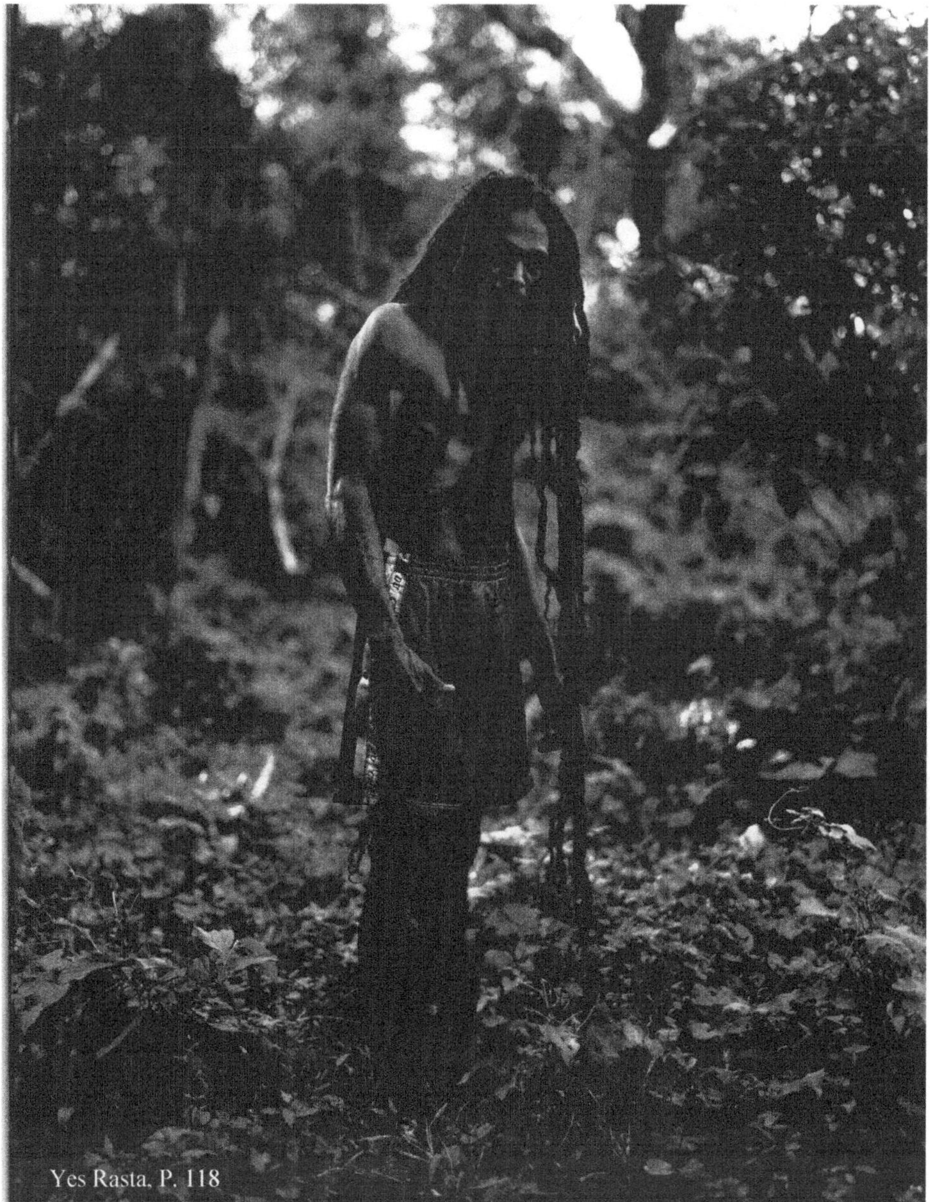

Yes Rasta, P. 118

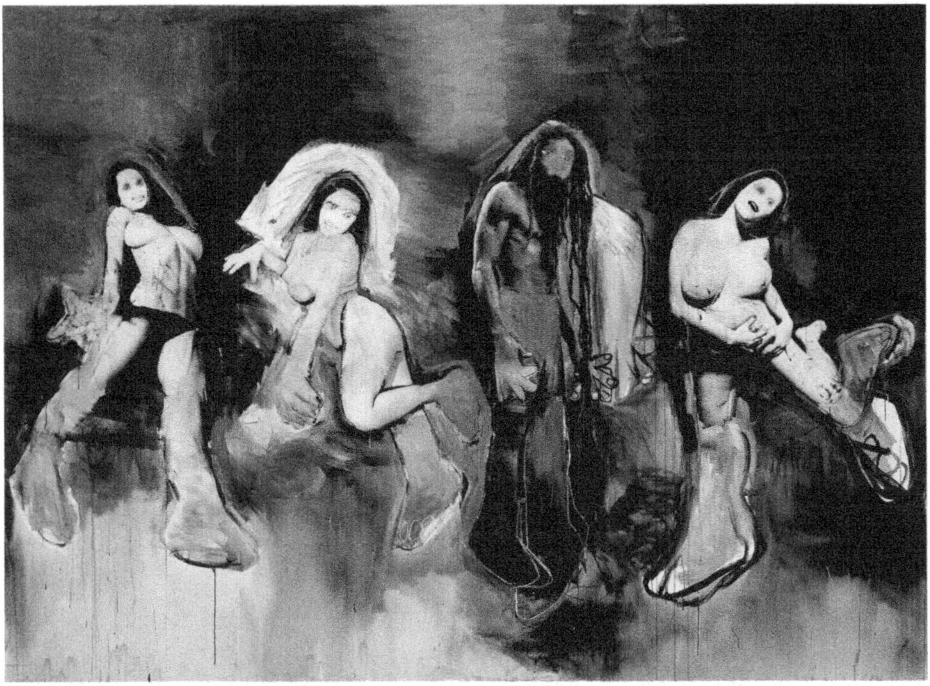

H

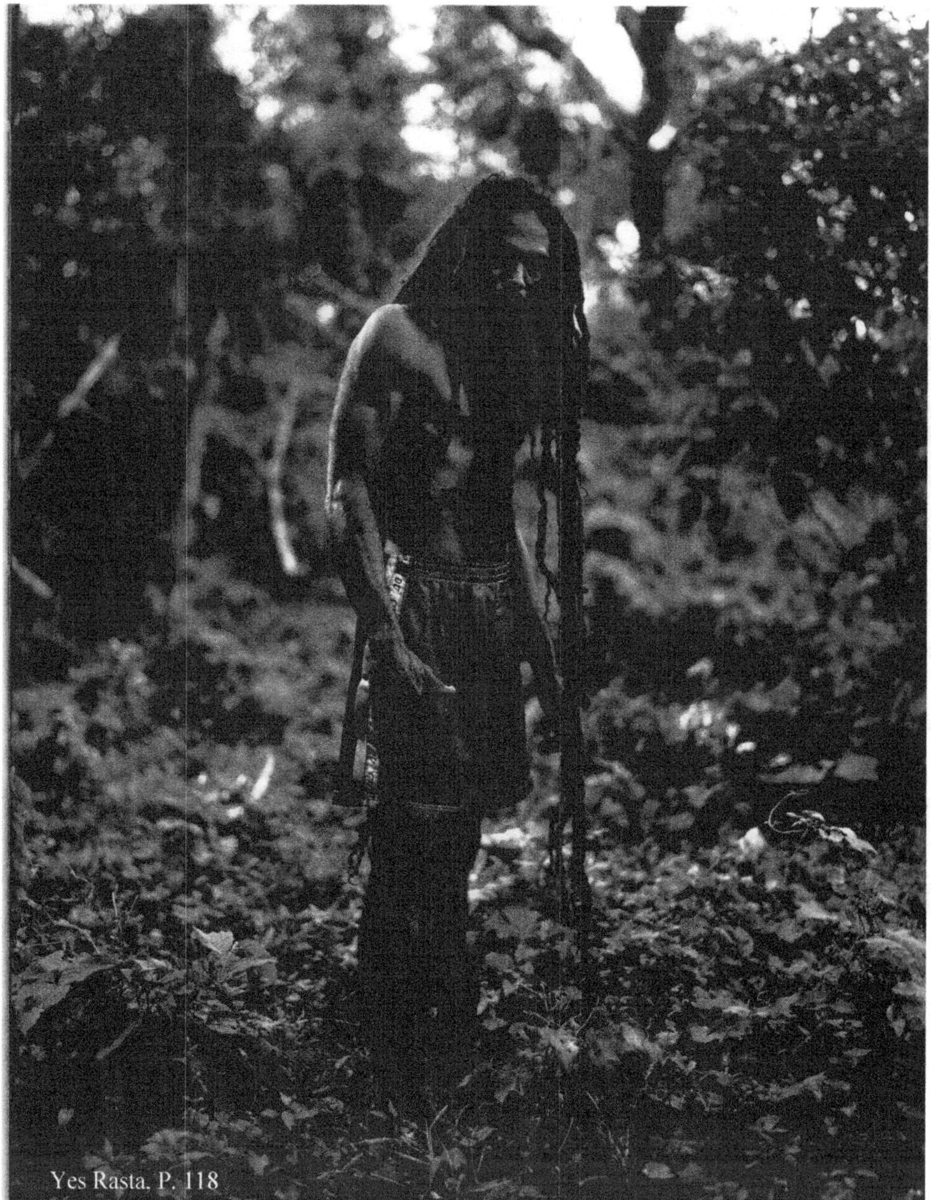

Yes Rasta. P. 118

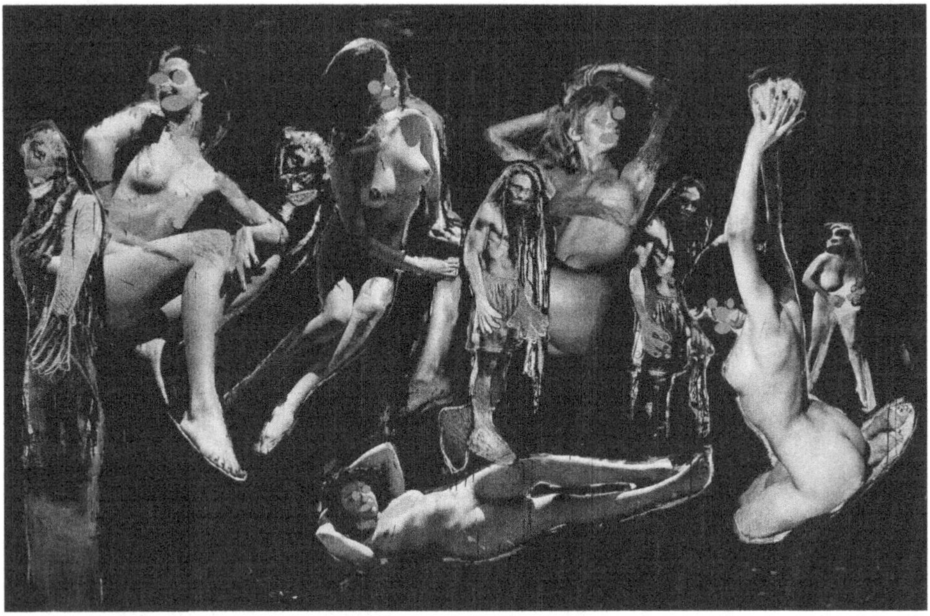

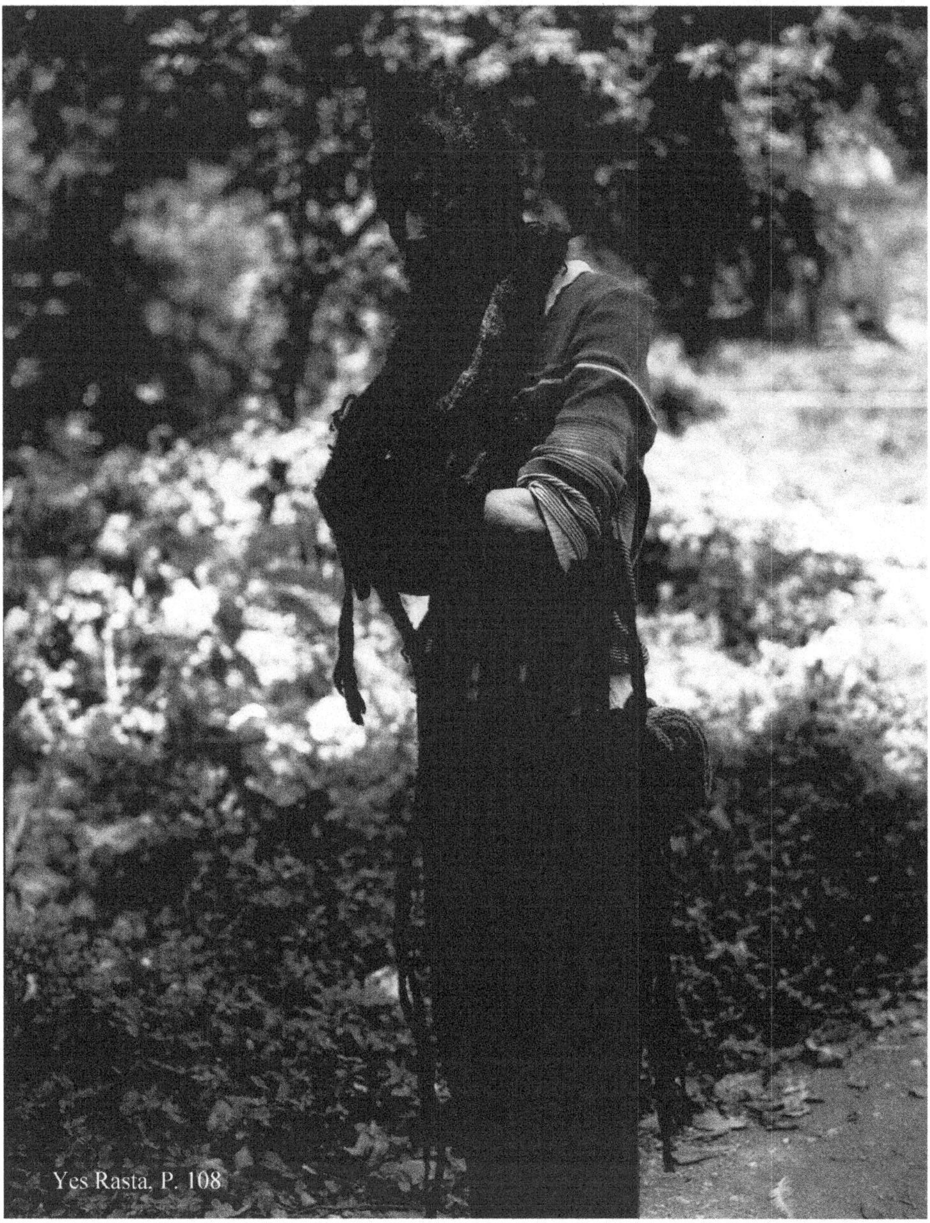

Yes Rasta, P. 108

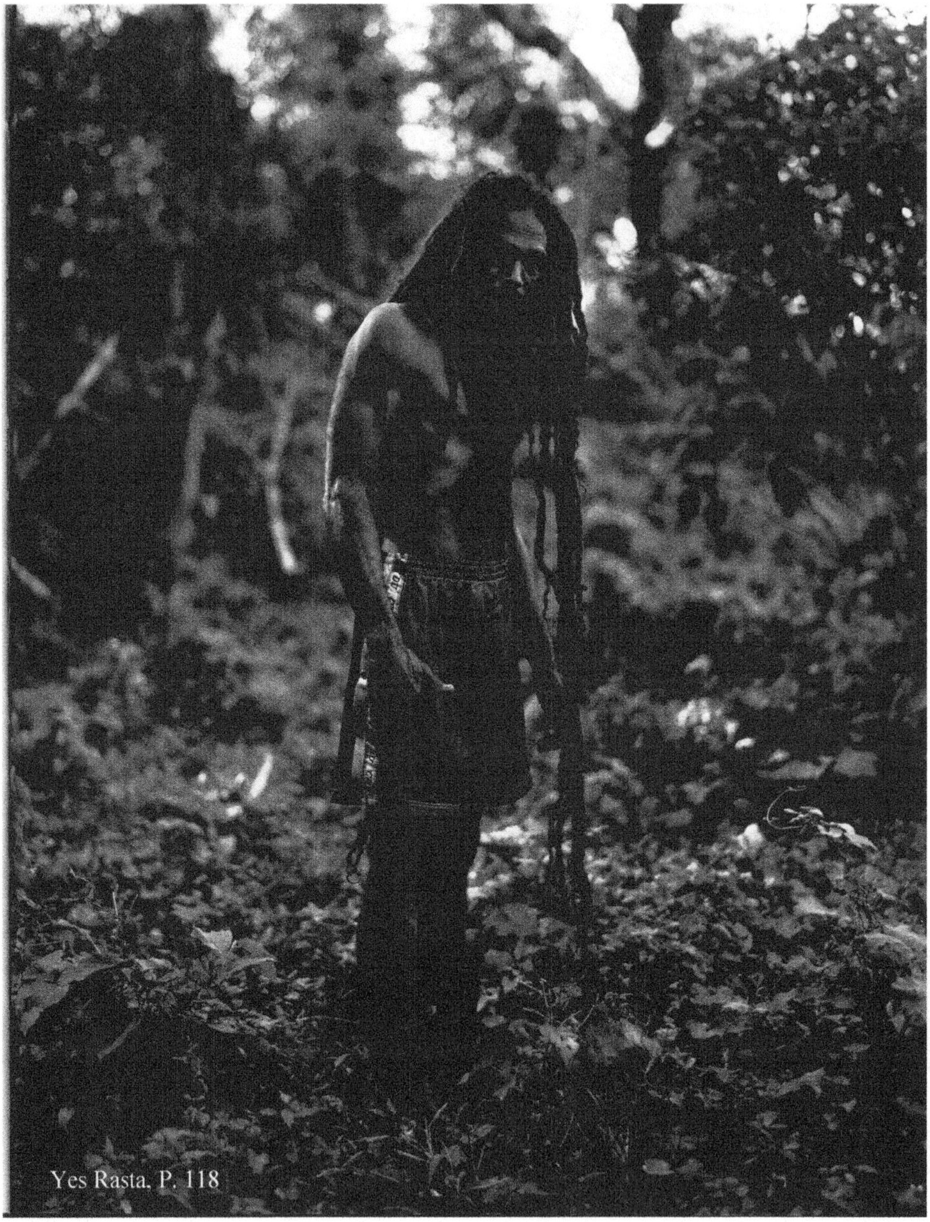

Yes Rasta, P. 118

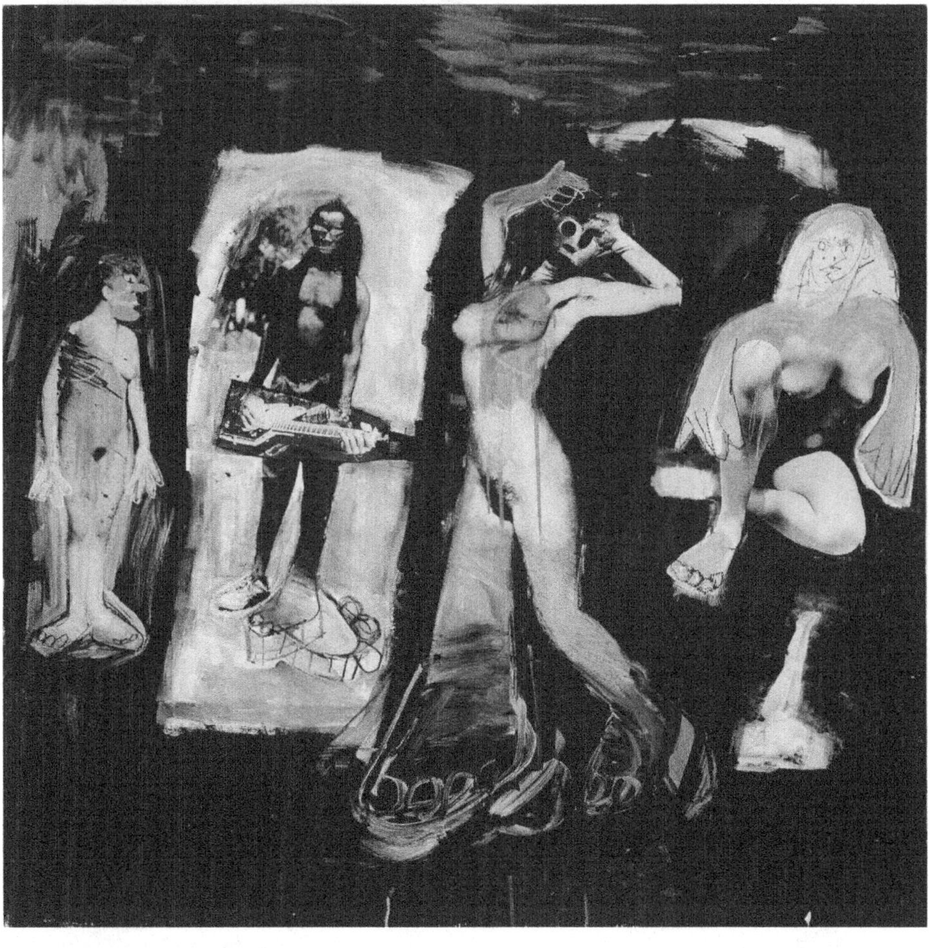

J

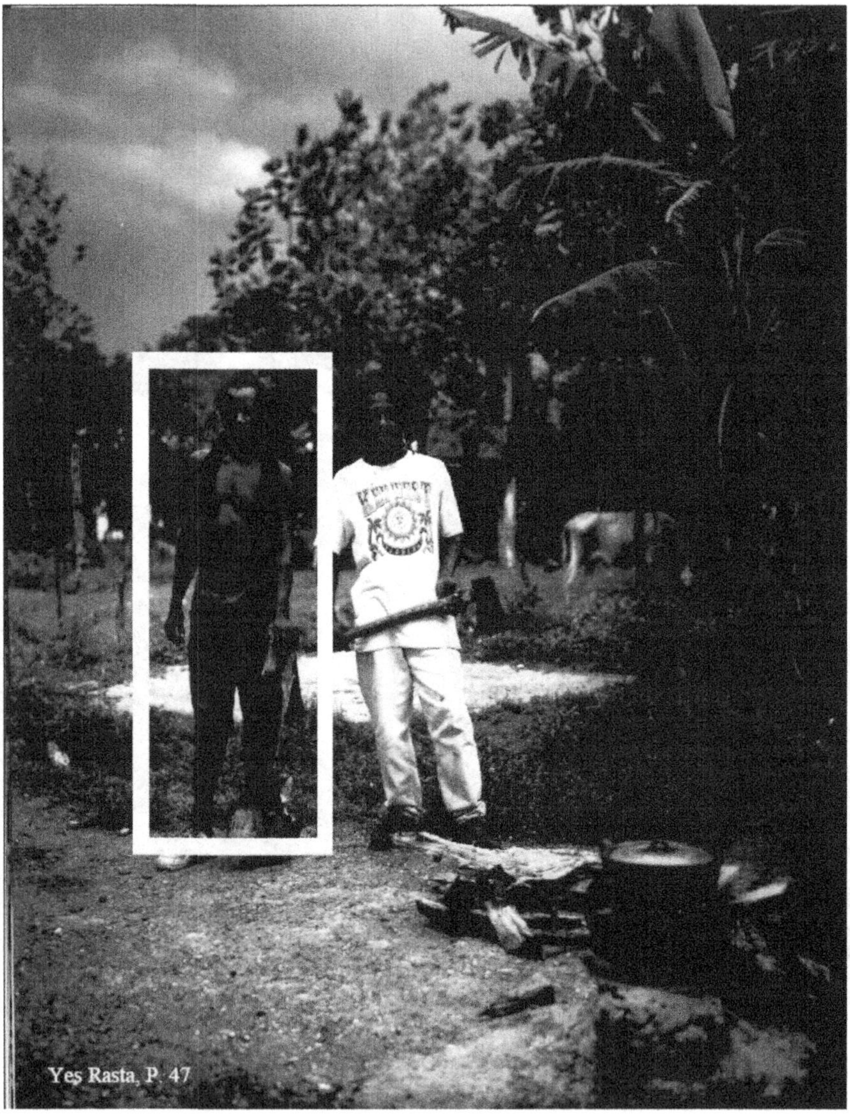
Yes Rasta, P. 47

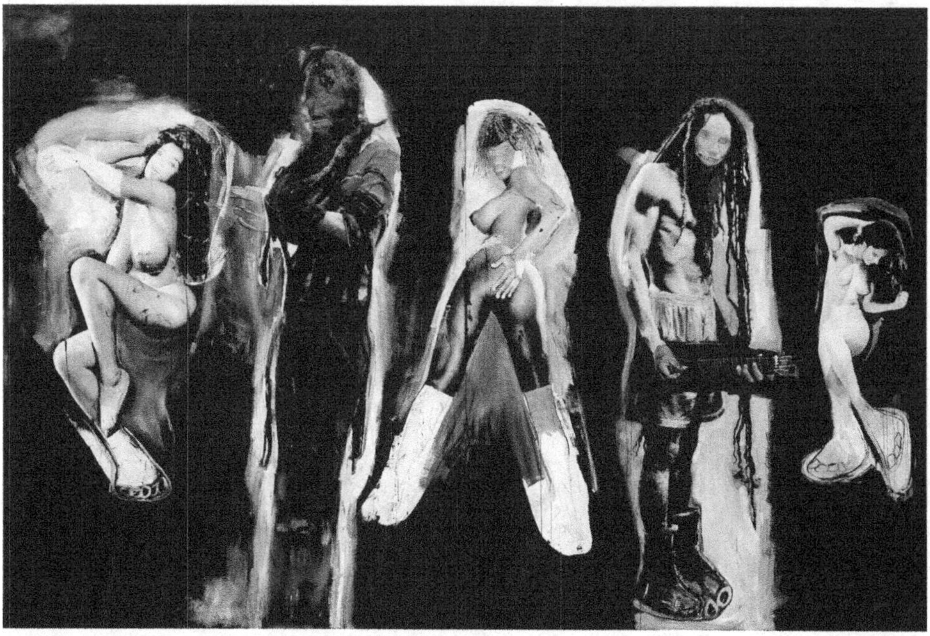

K

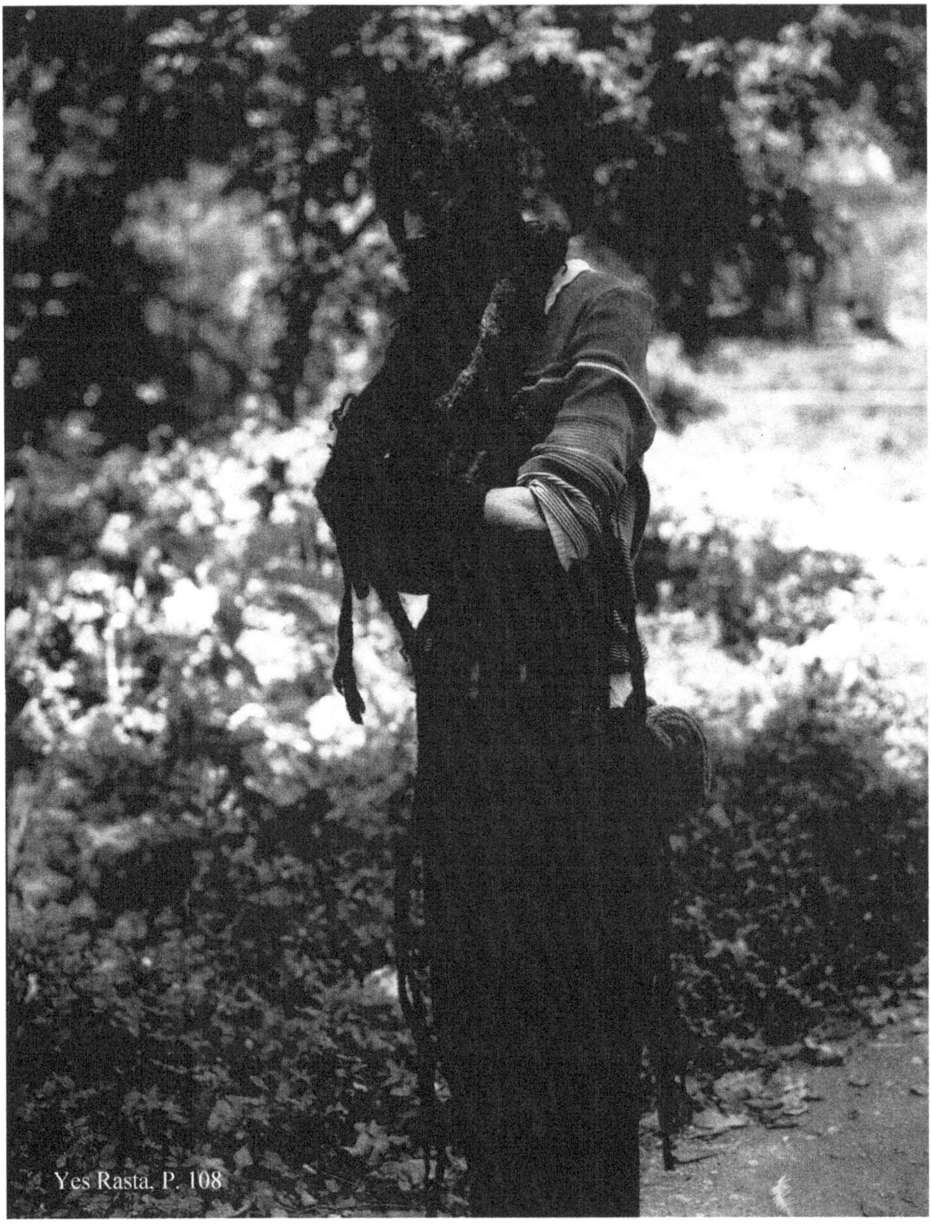

Yes Rasta. P. 108

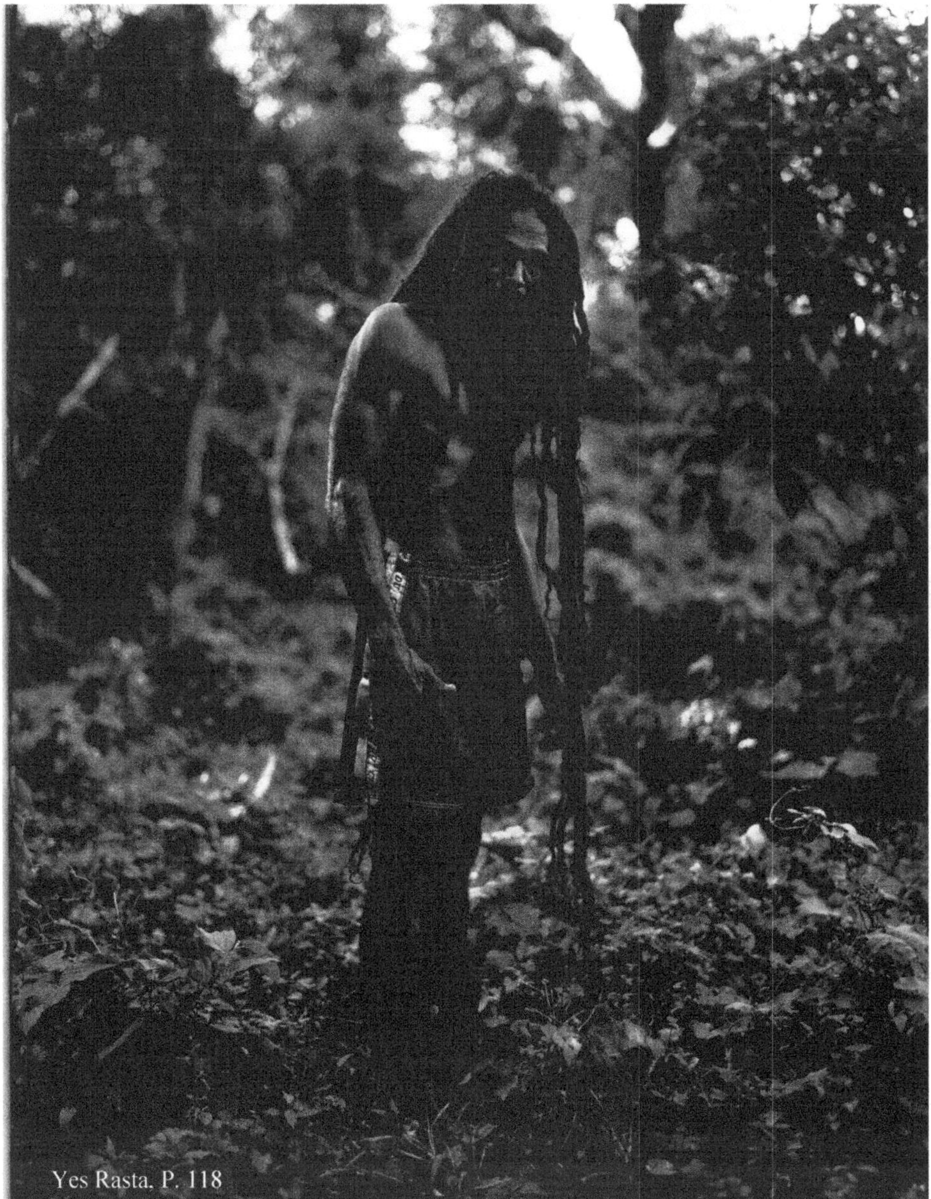

Yes Rasta. P. 118

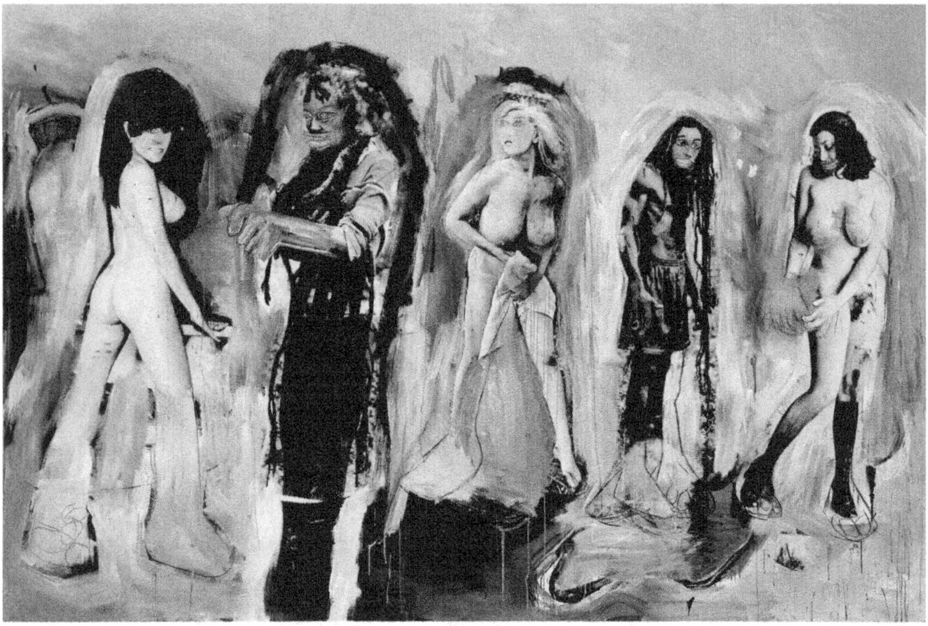

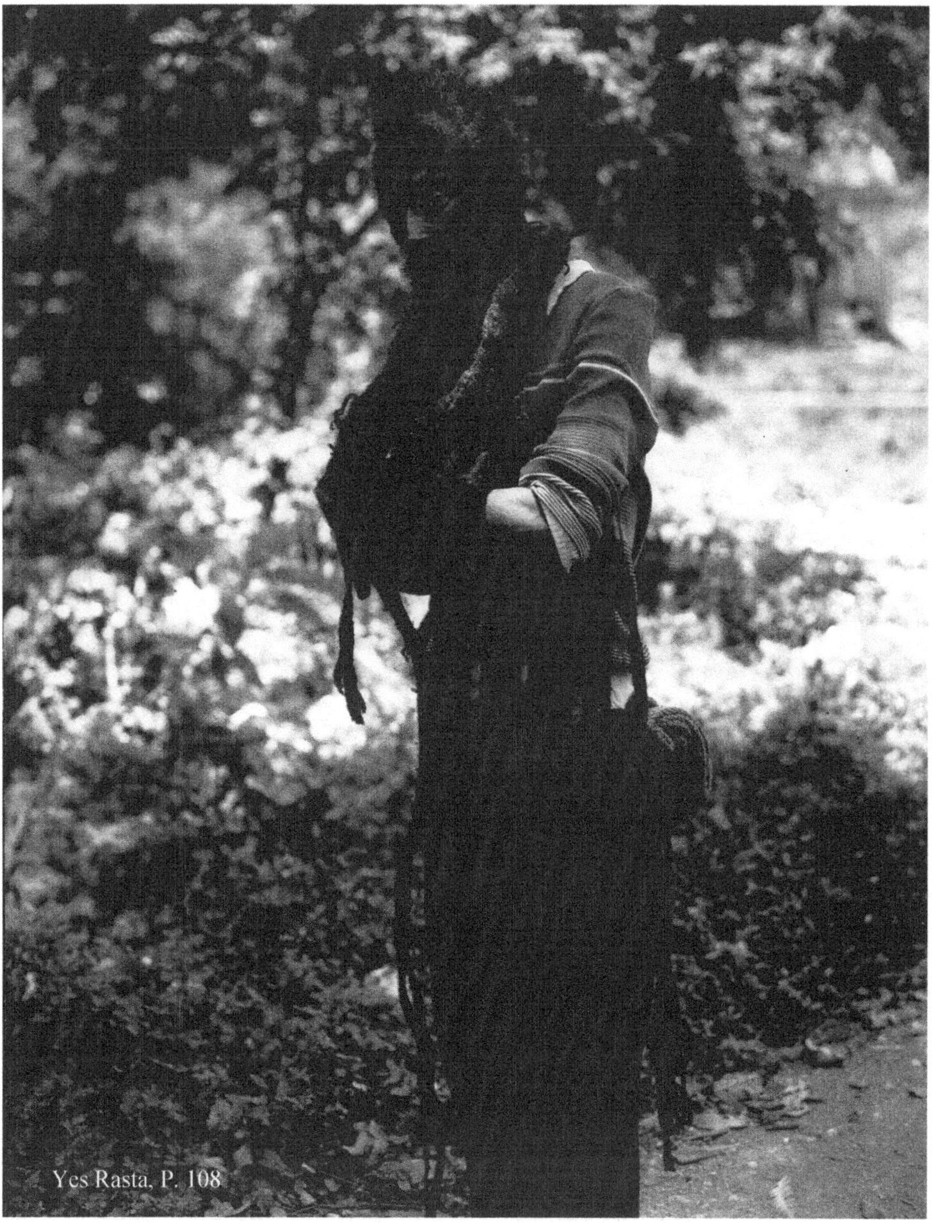
Yes Rasta, P. 108

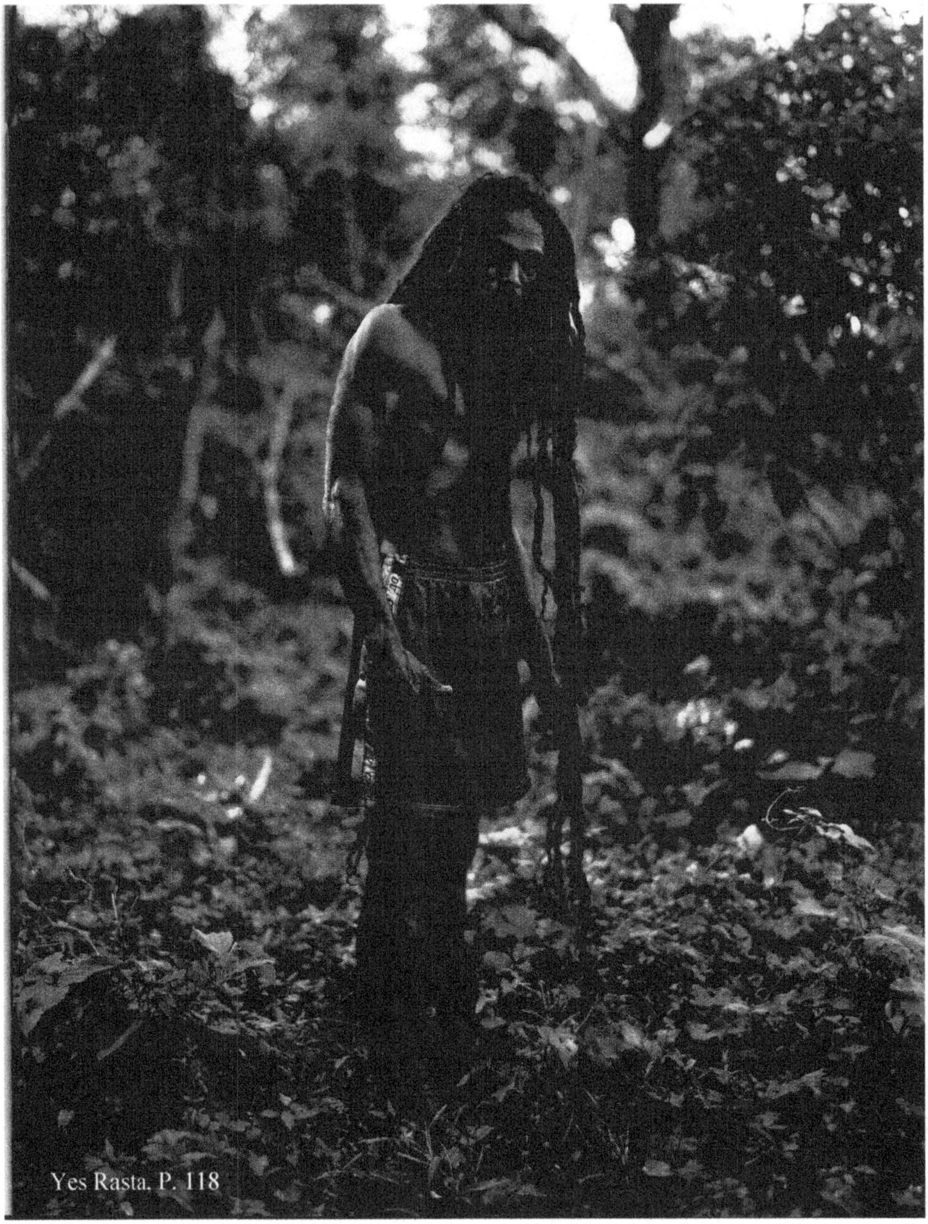

Yes Rasta, P. 118

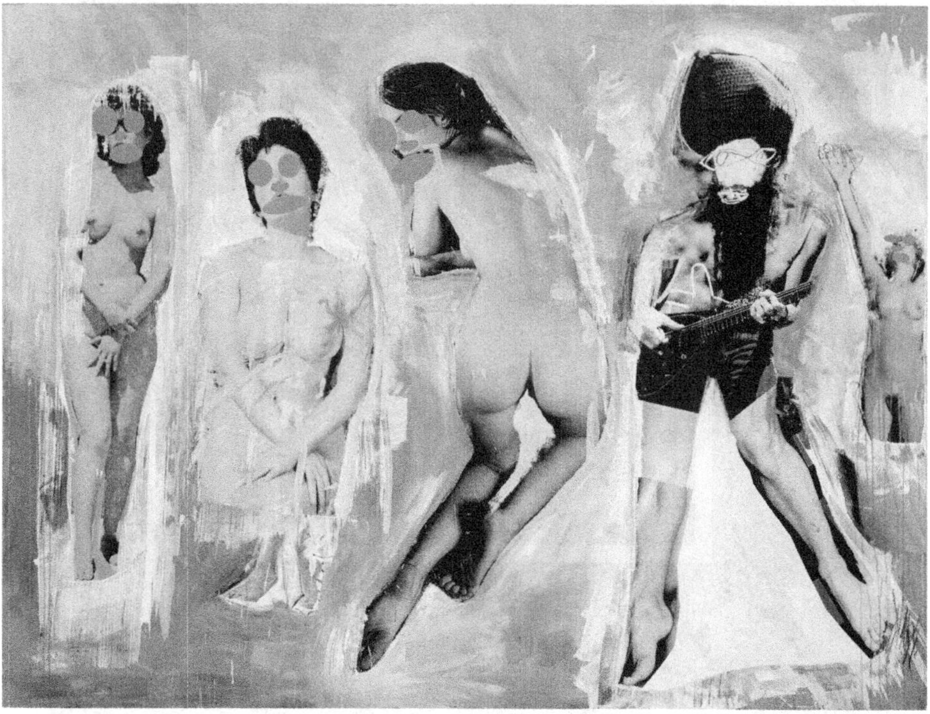

M

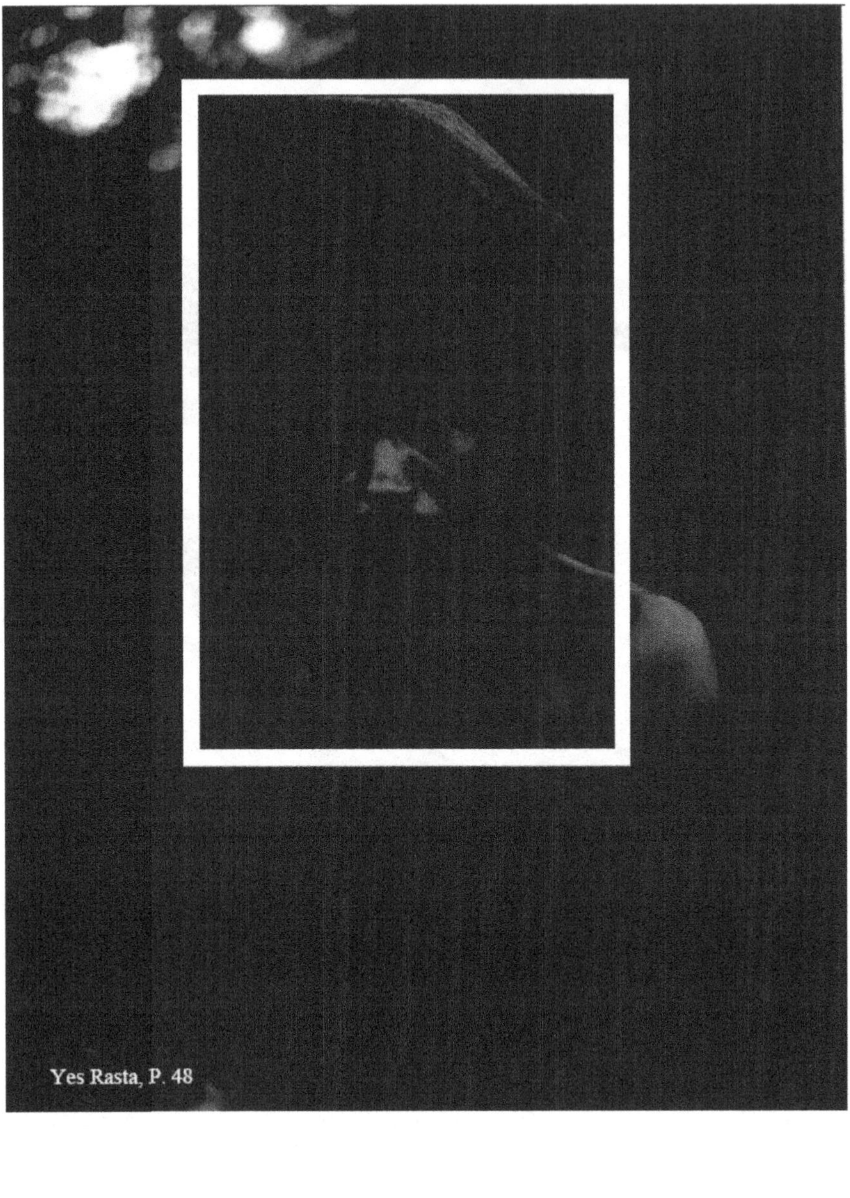
Yes Rasta, P. 48

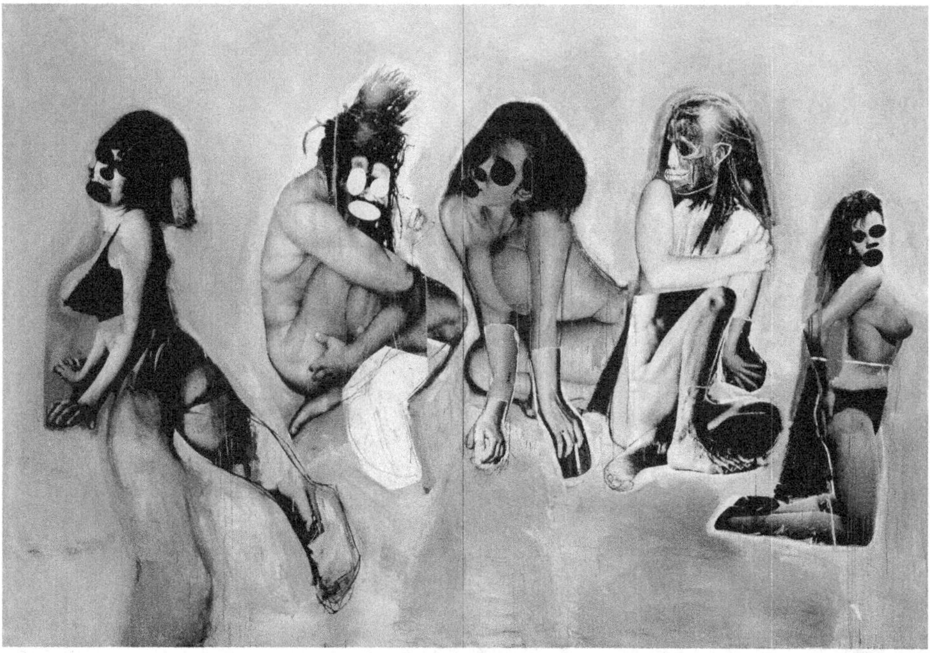

N

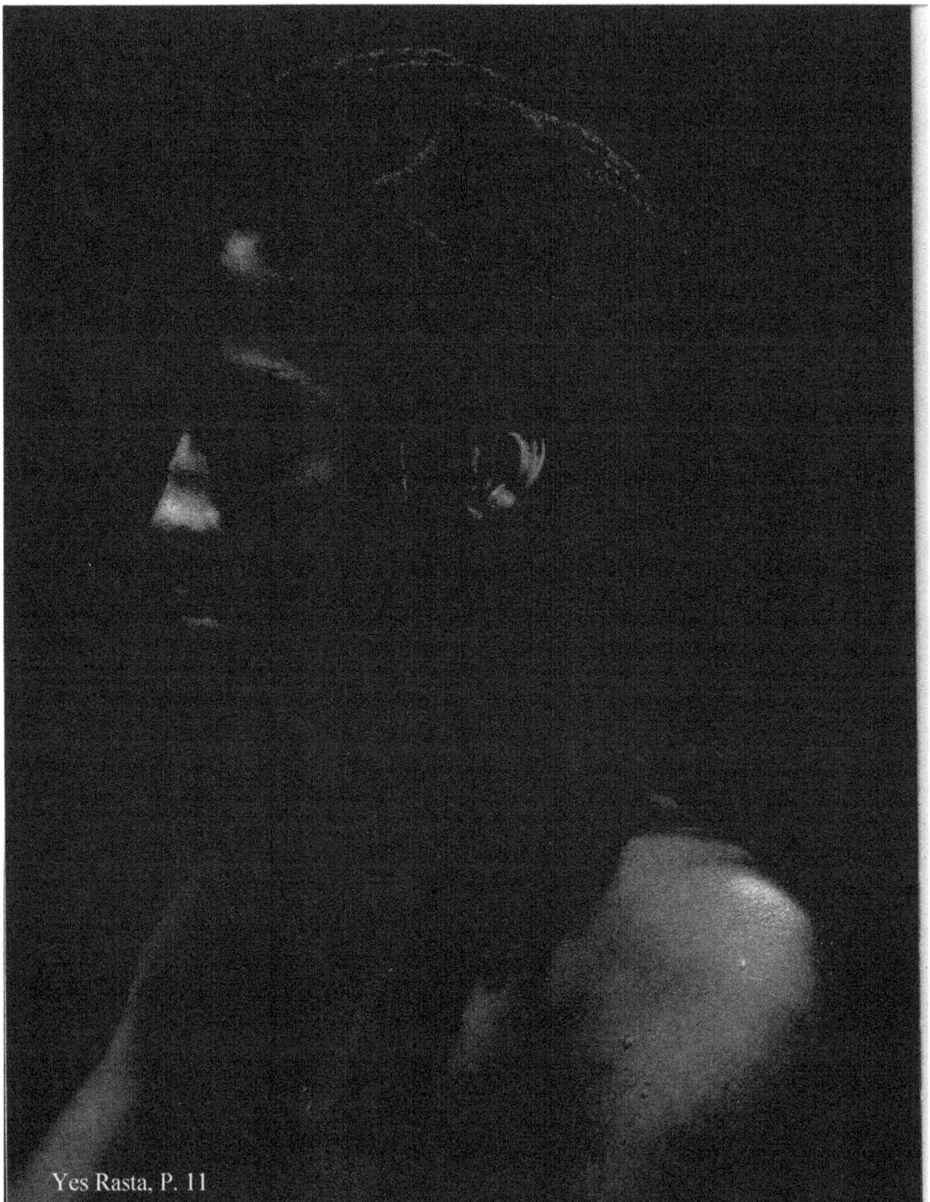
Yes Rasta, P. 11

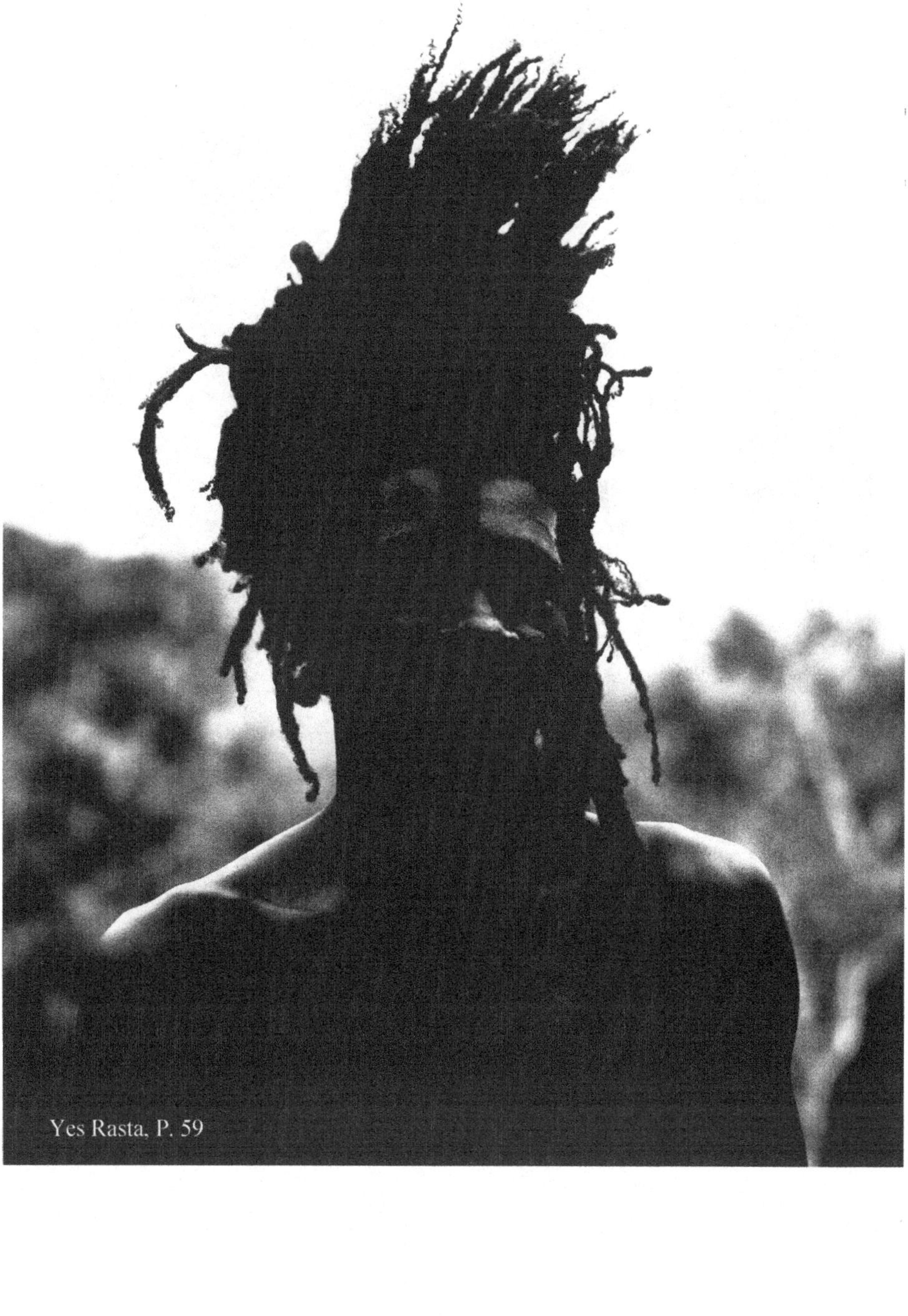

Yes Rasta, P. 59

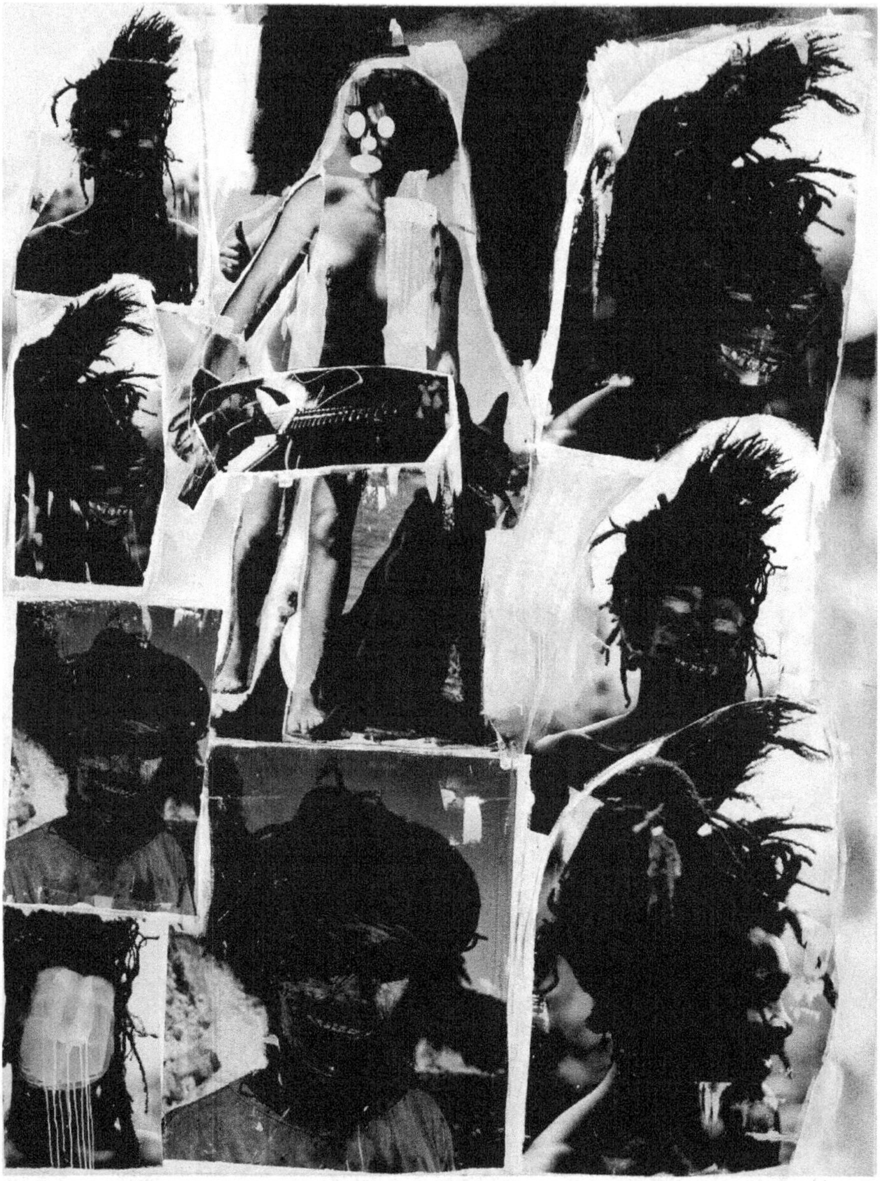

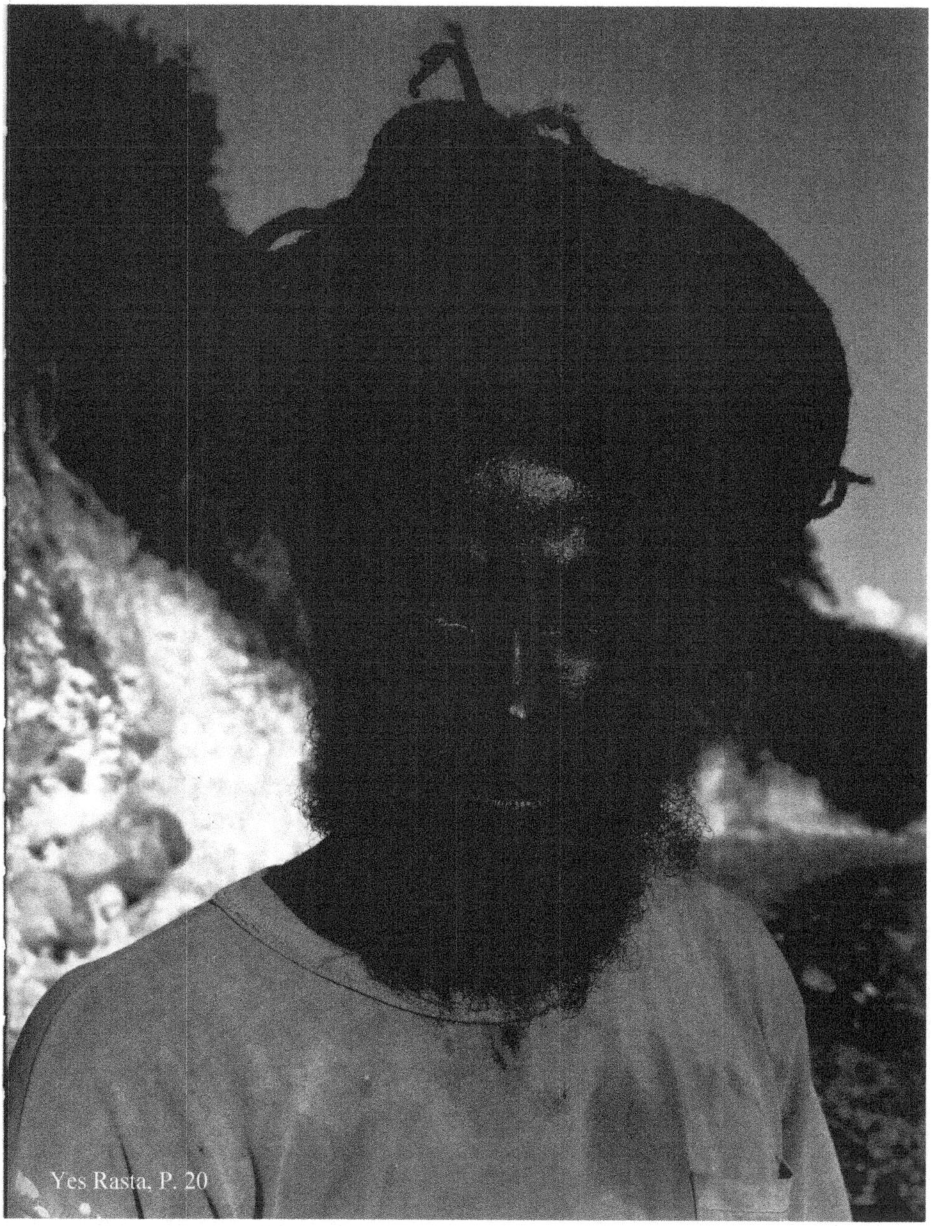
Yes Rasta, P. 20

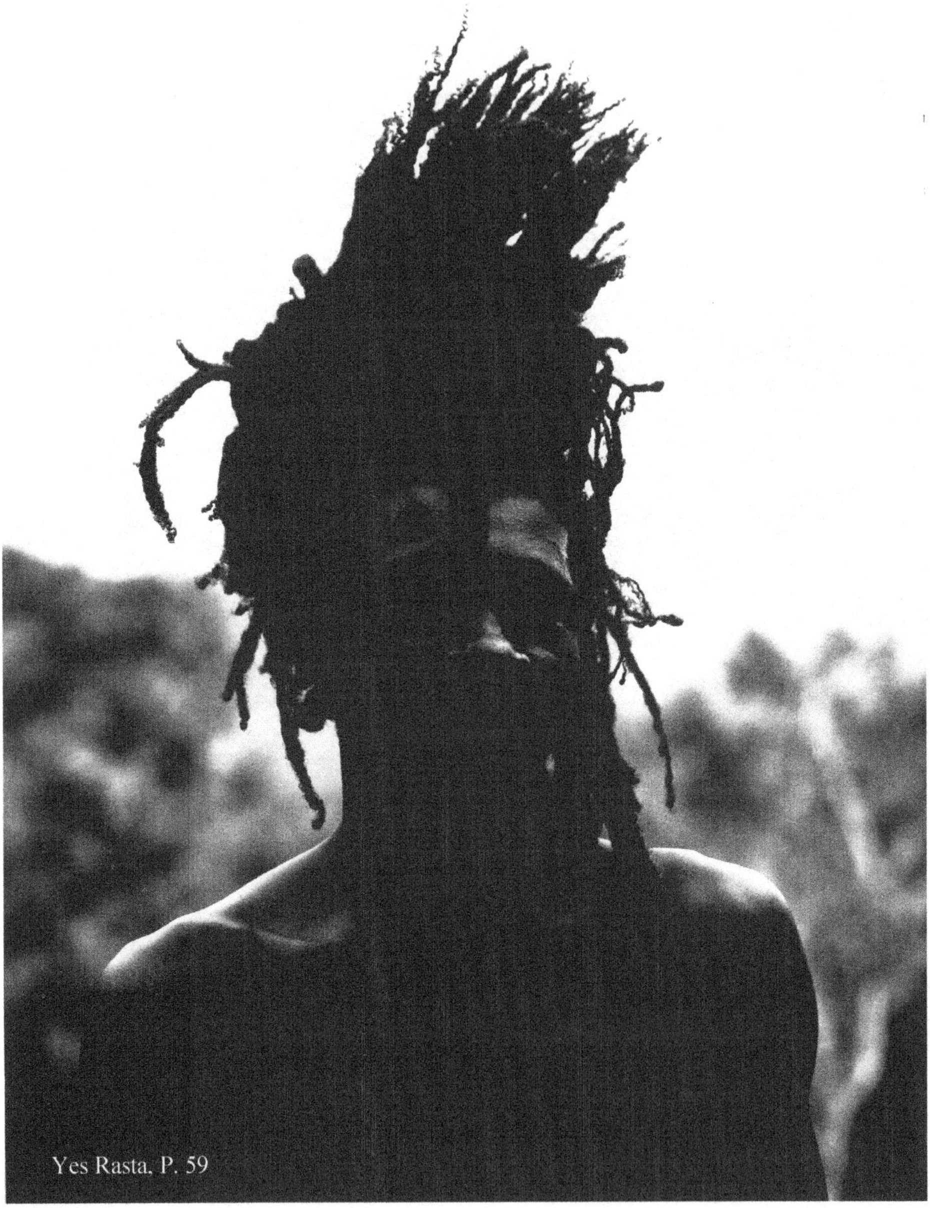
Yes Rasta, P. 59

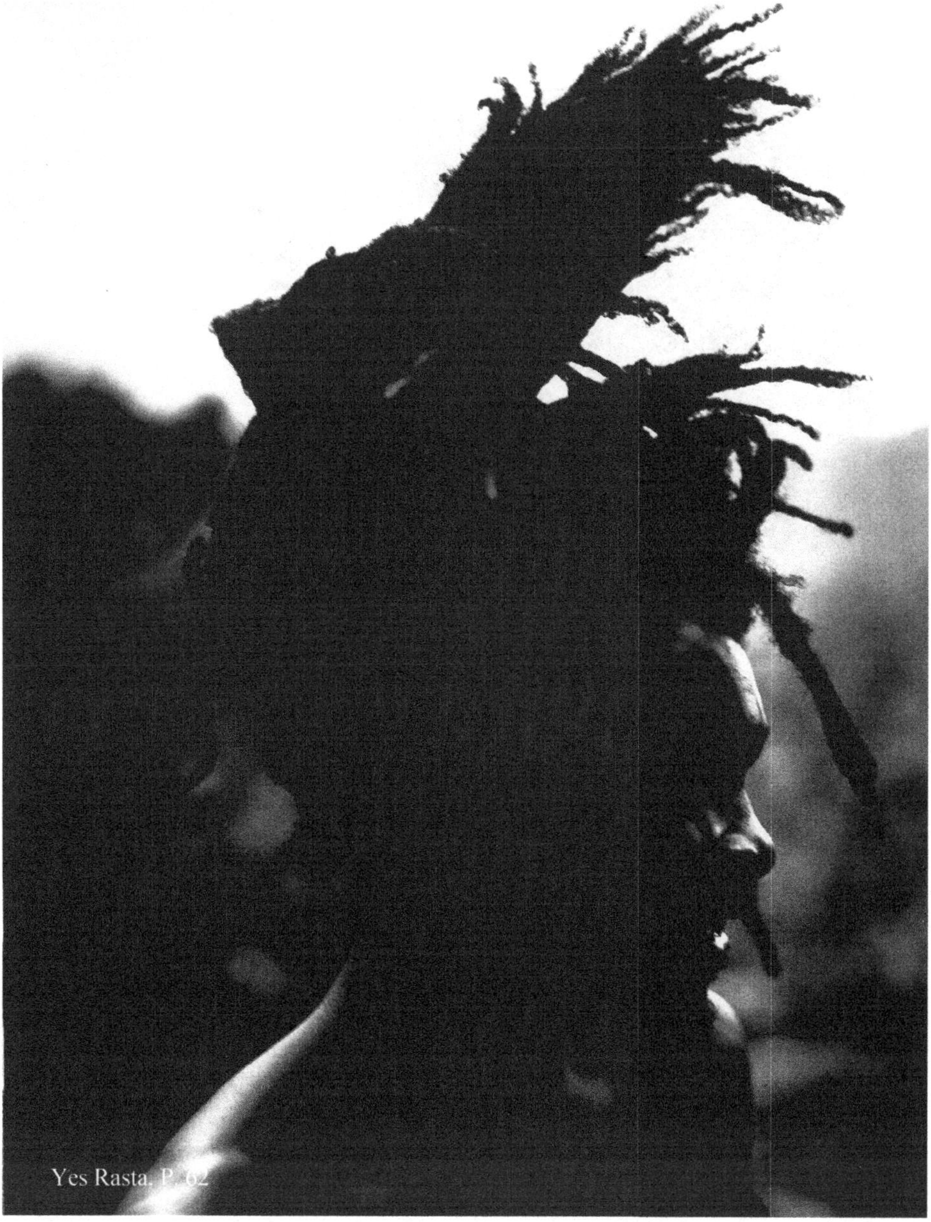
Yes Rasta, P. 62

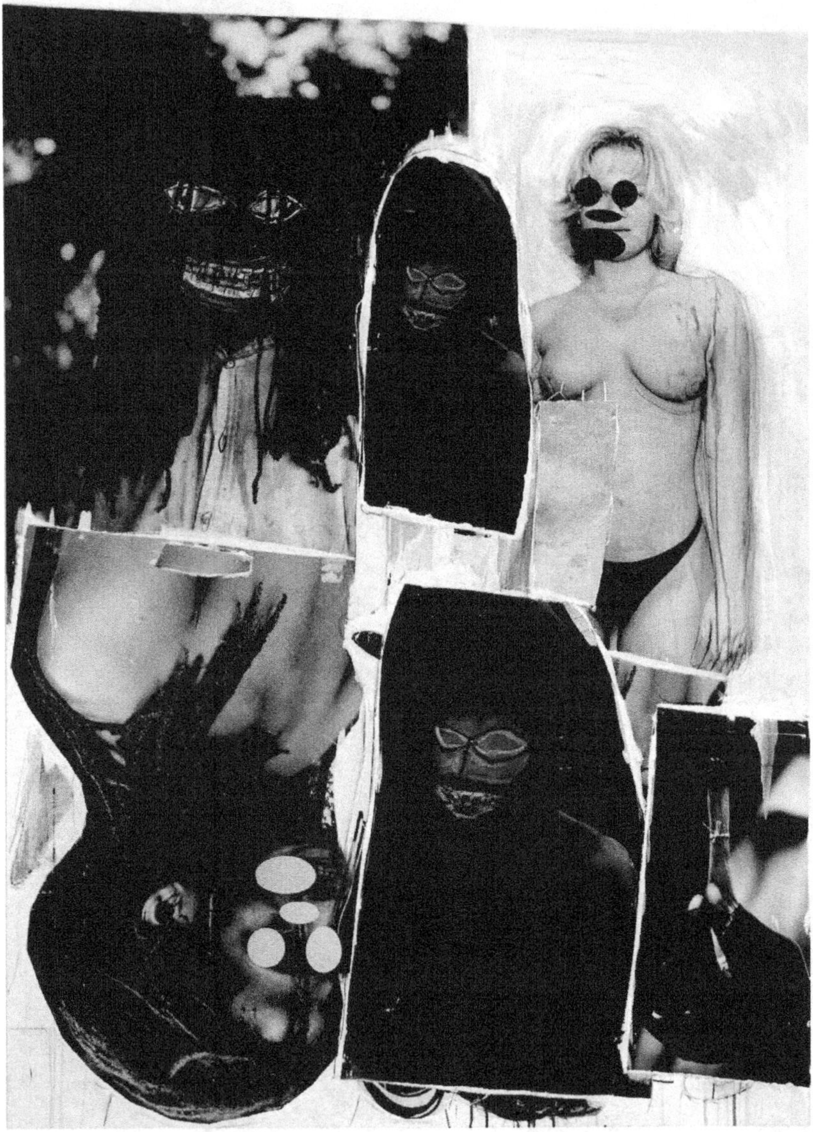

P

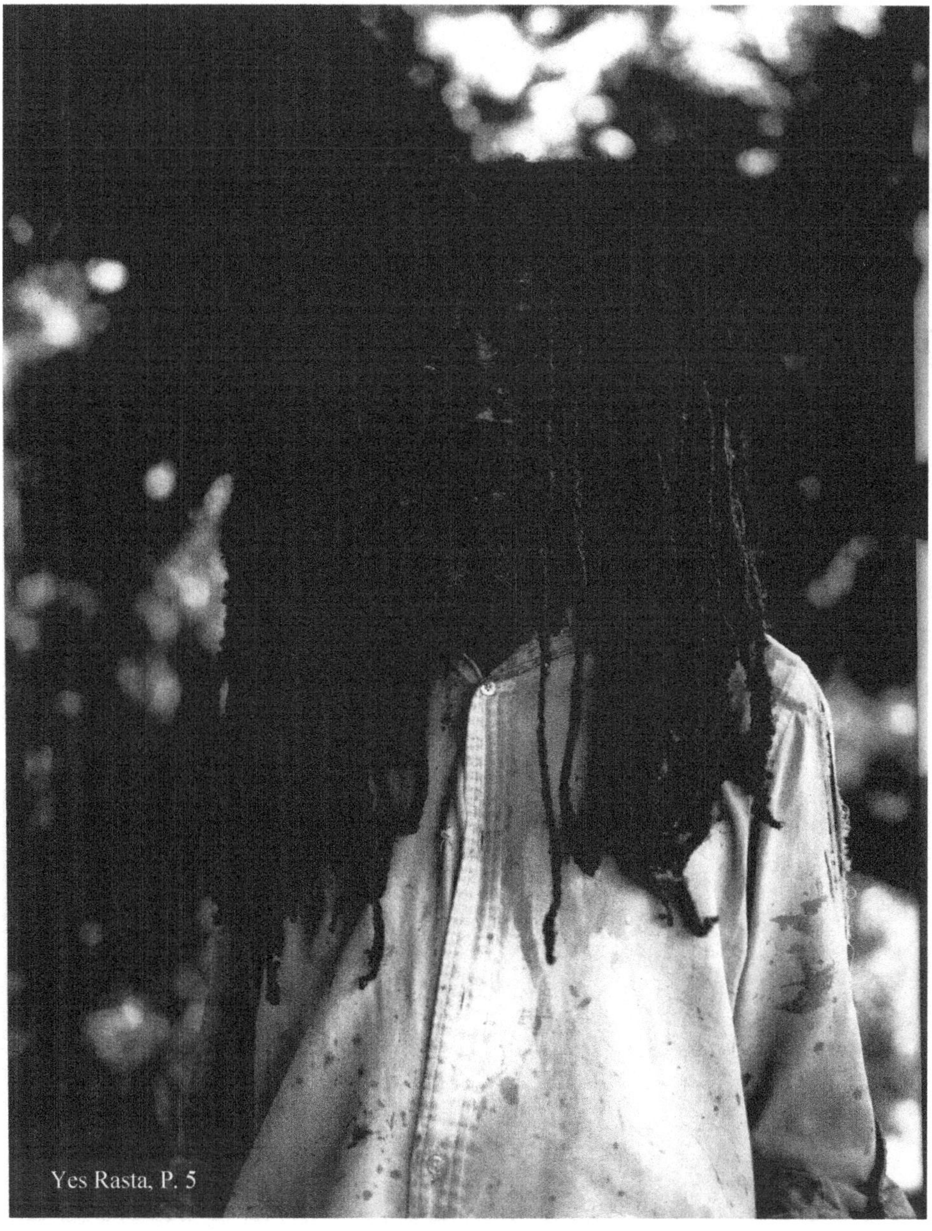

Yes Rasta, P. 5

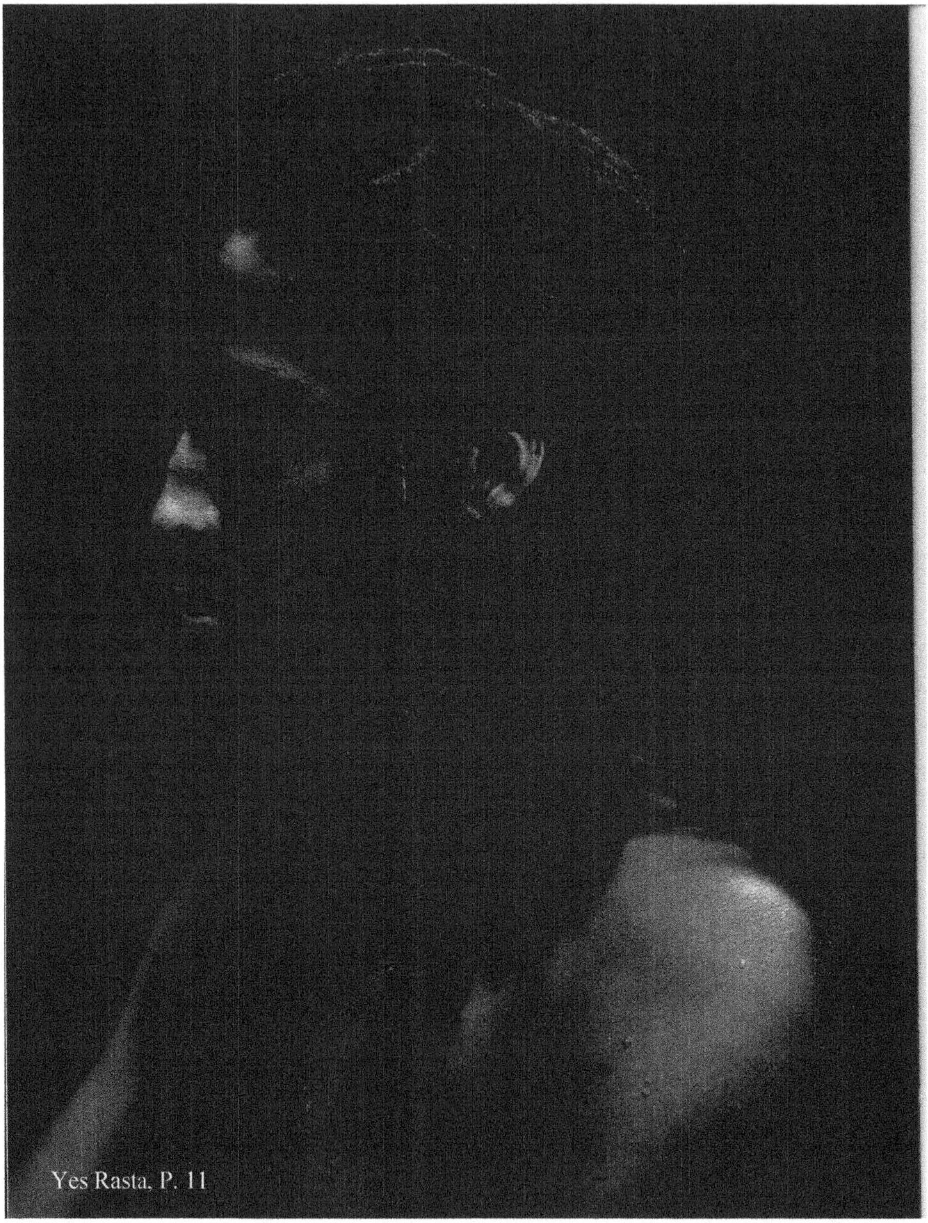

Yes Rasta, P. 11

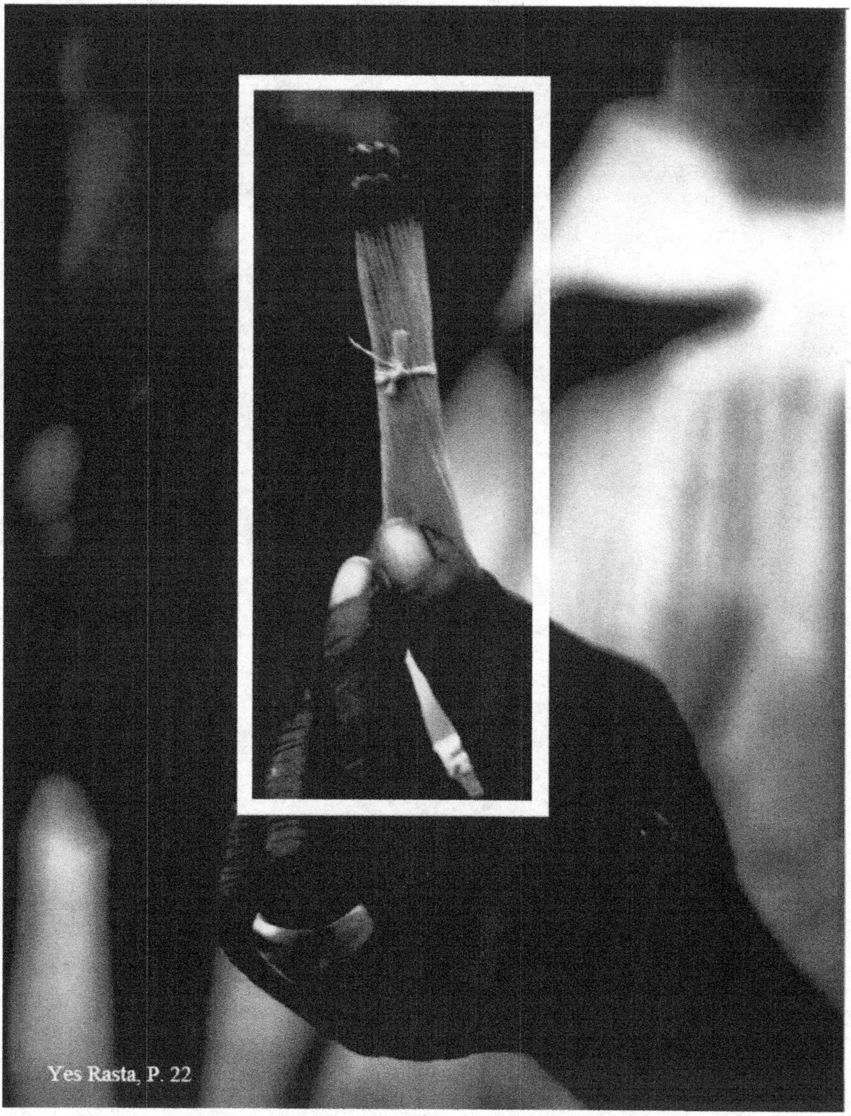
Yes Rasta, P. 22

Yes Rasta, P. 48

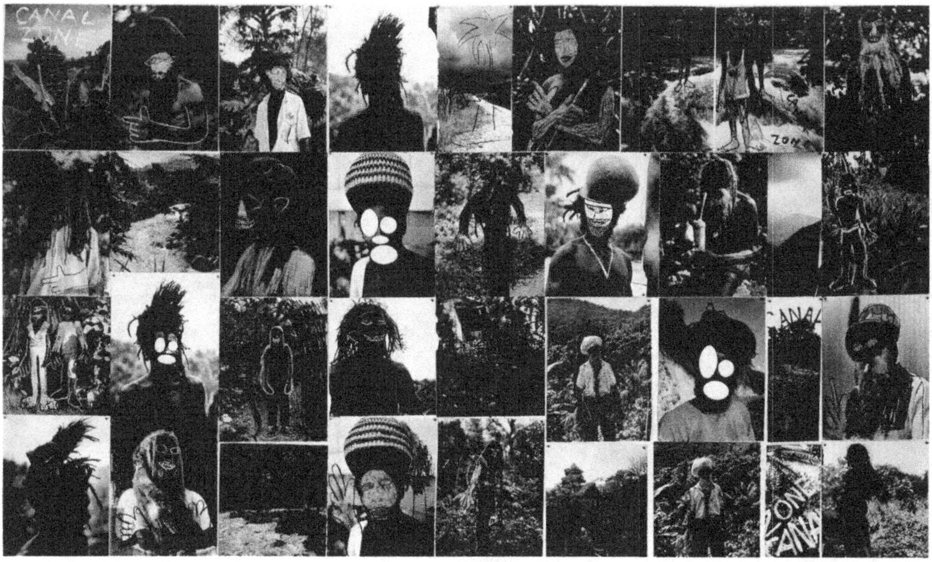

Q

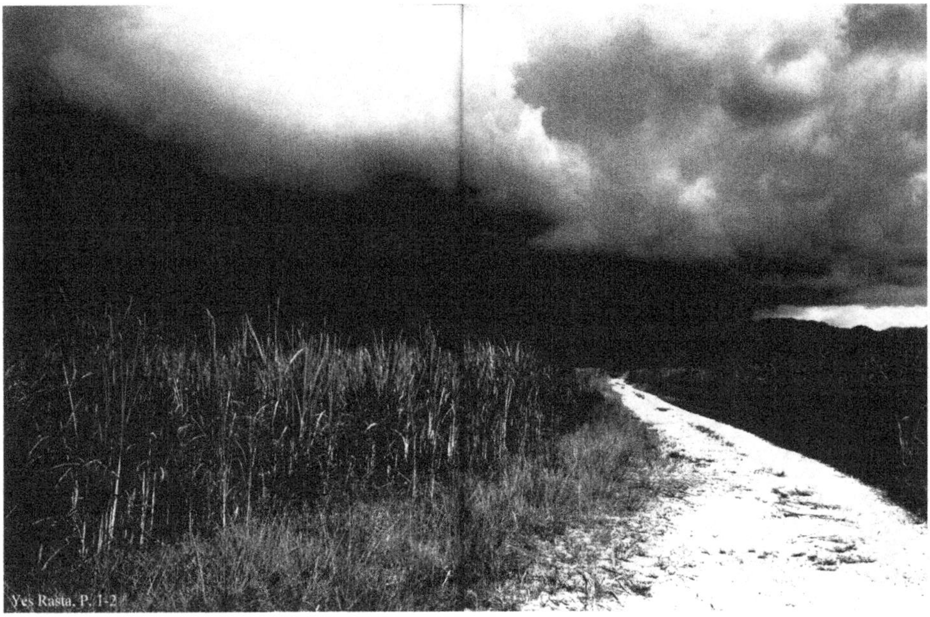
Yes Rasta, P. 1-2

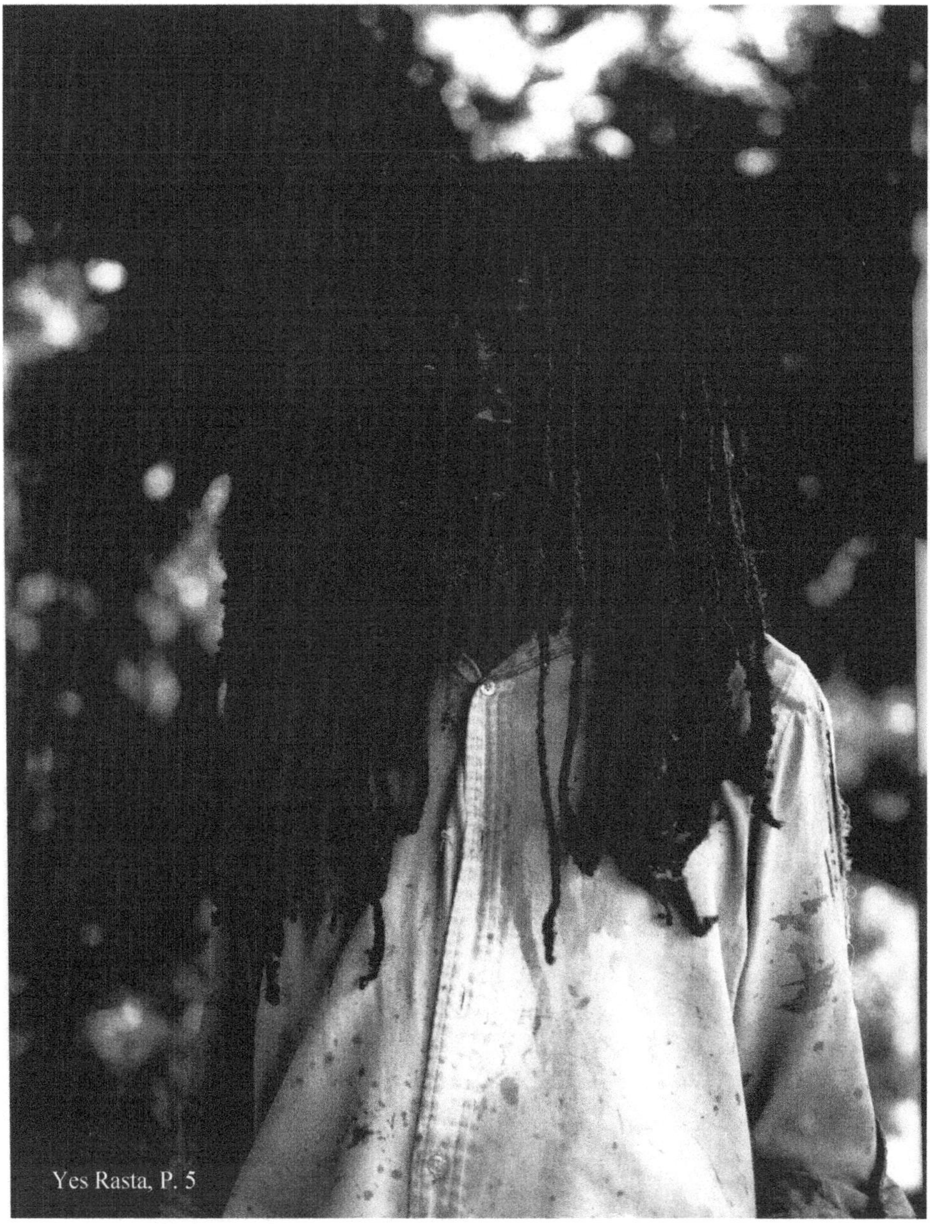

Yes Rasta, P. 5

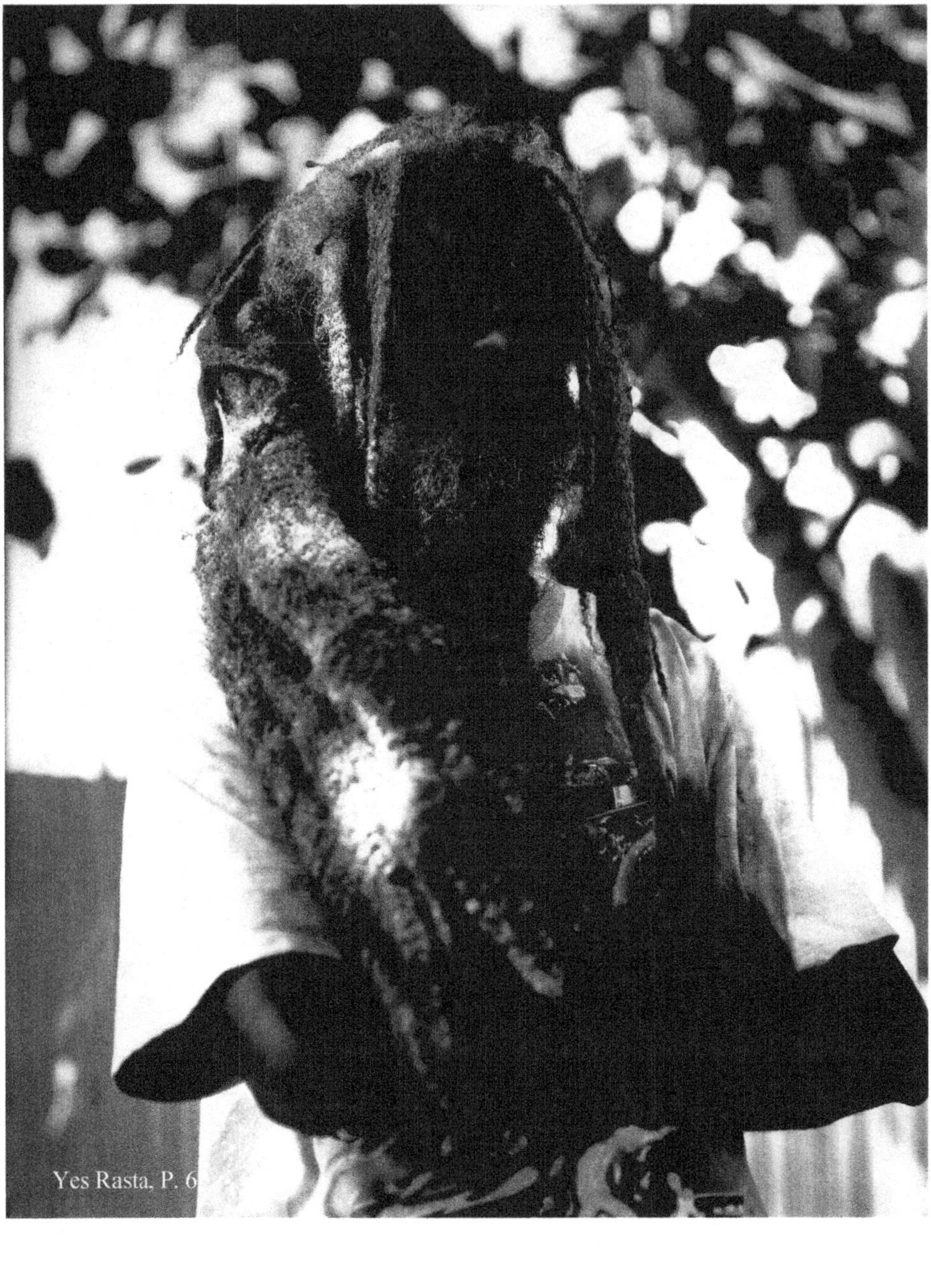

Yes Rasta, P. 6

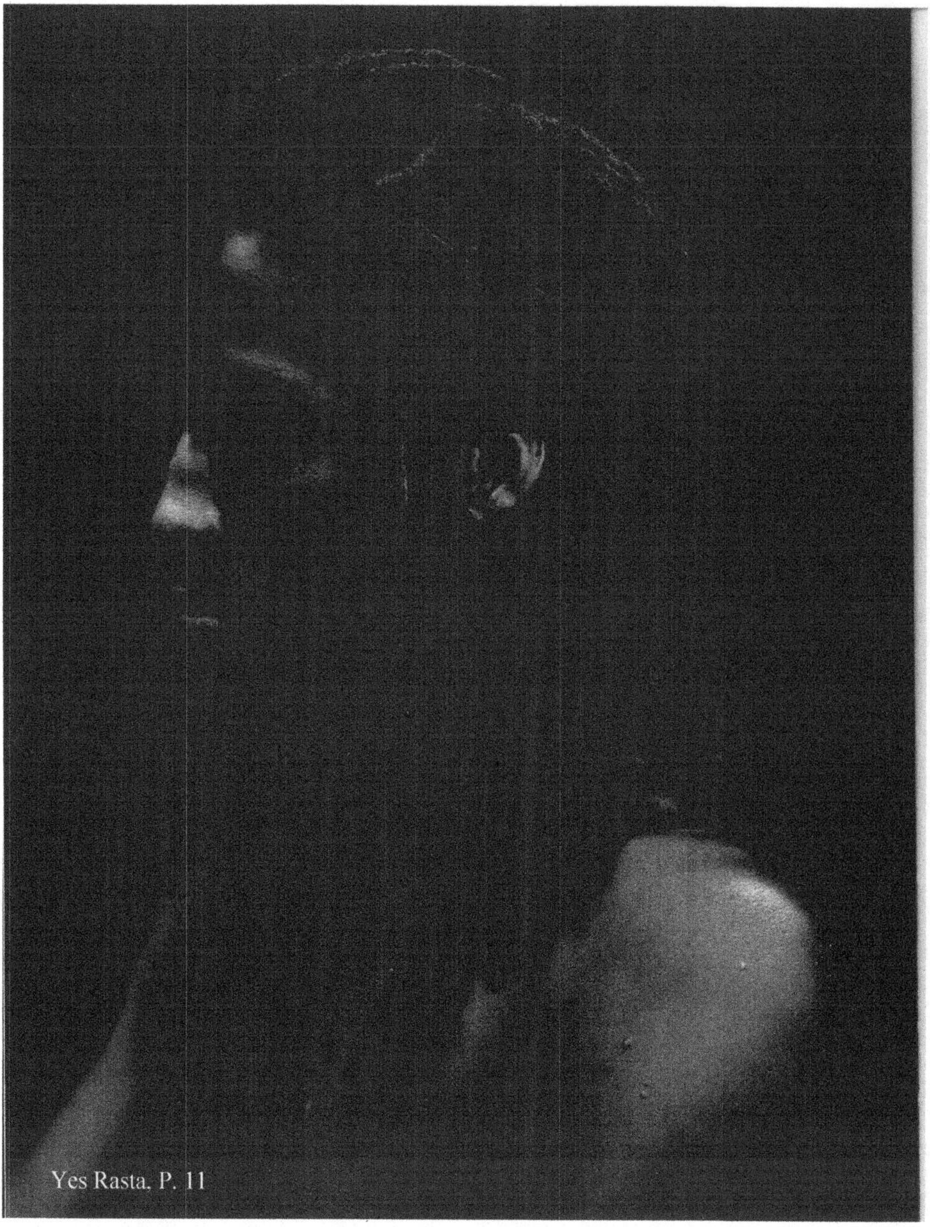
Yes Rasta, P. 11

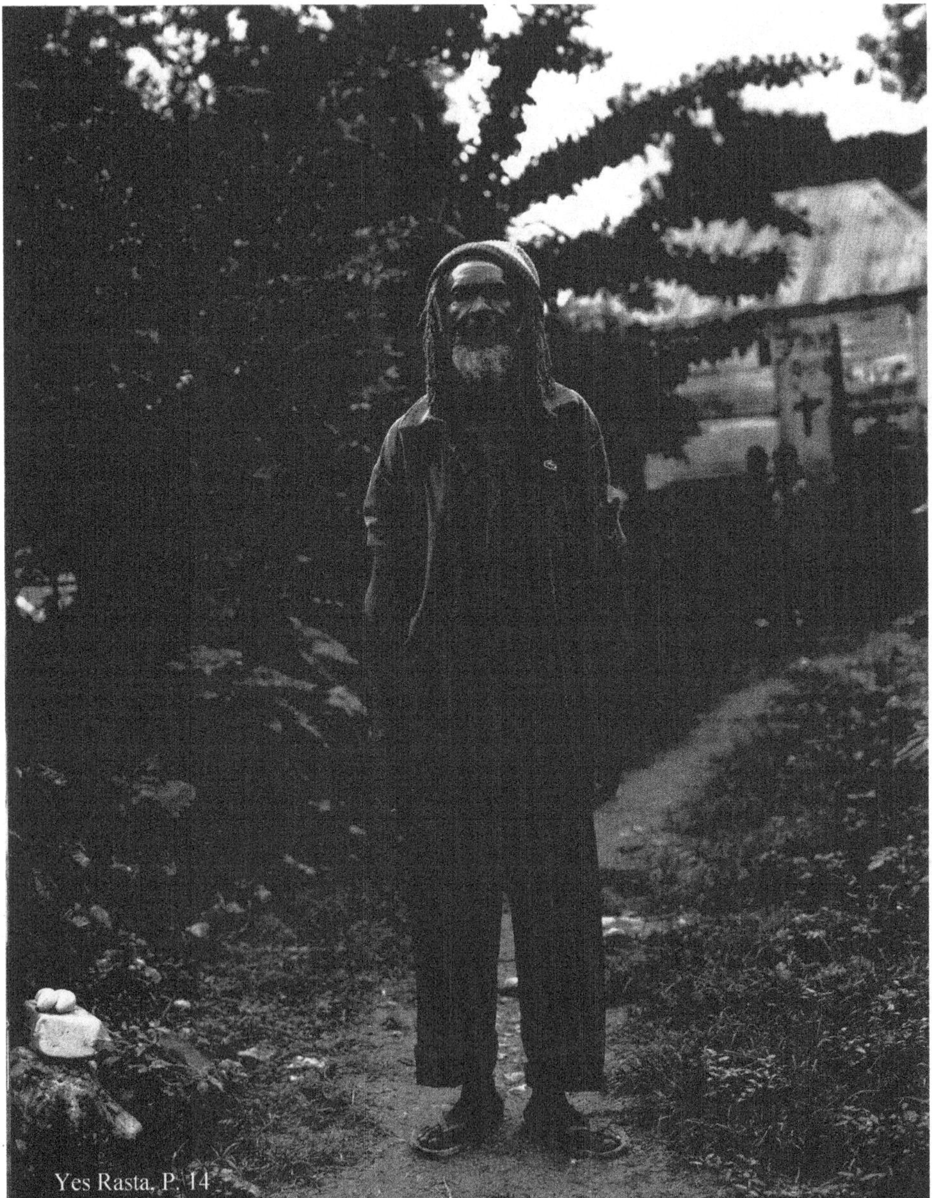

Yes Rasta, P. 14

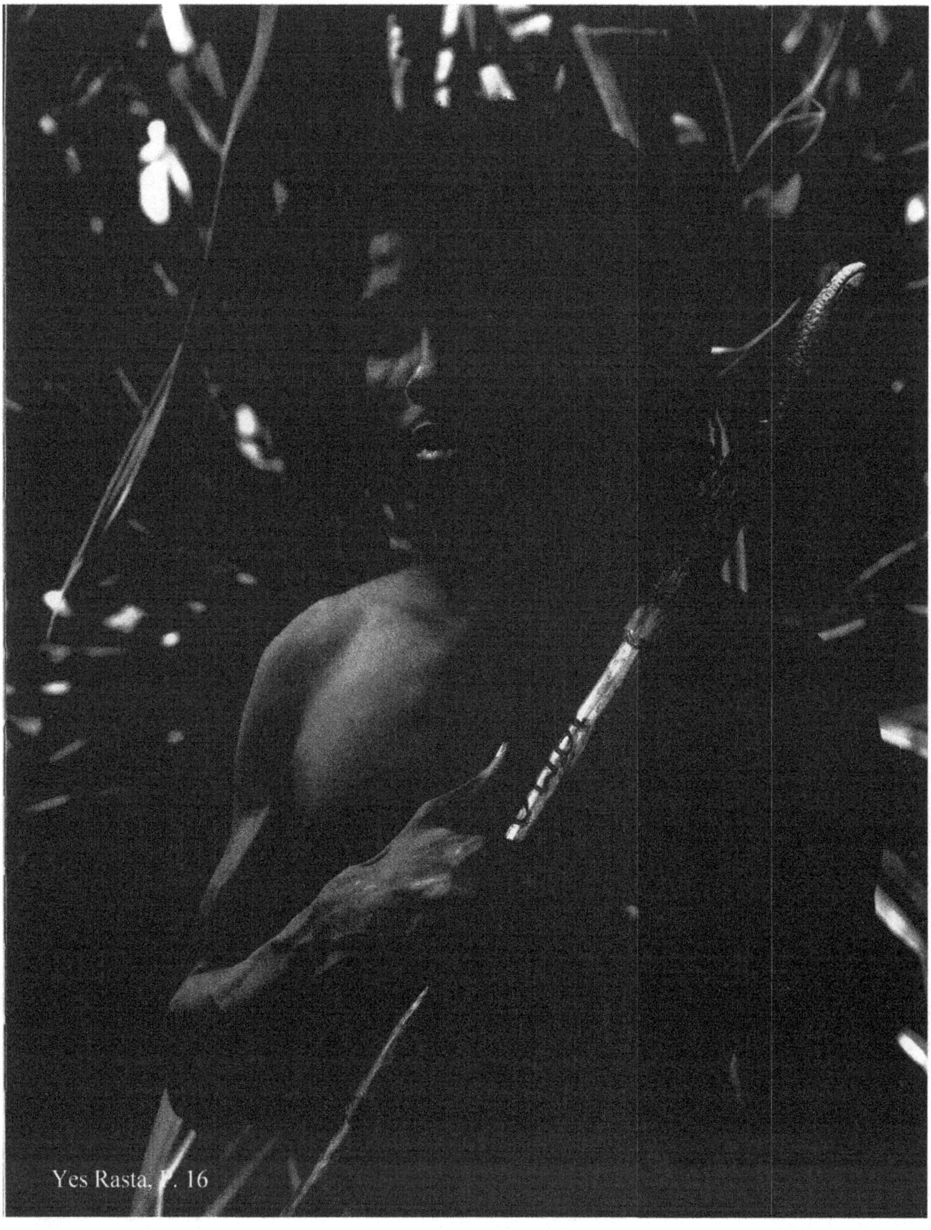
Yes Rasta, P. 16

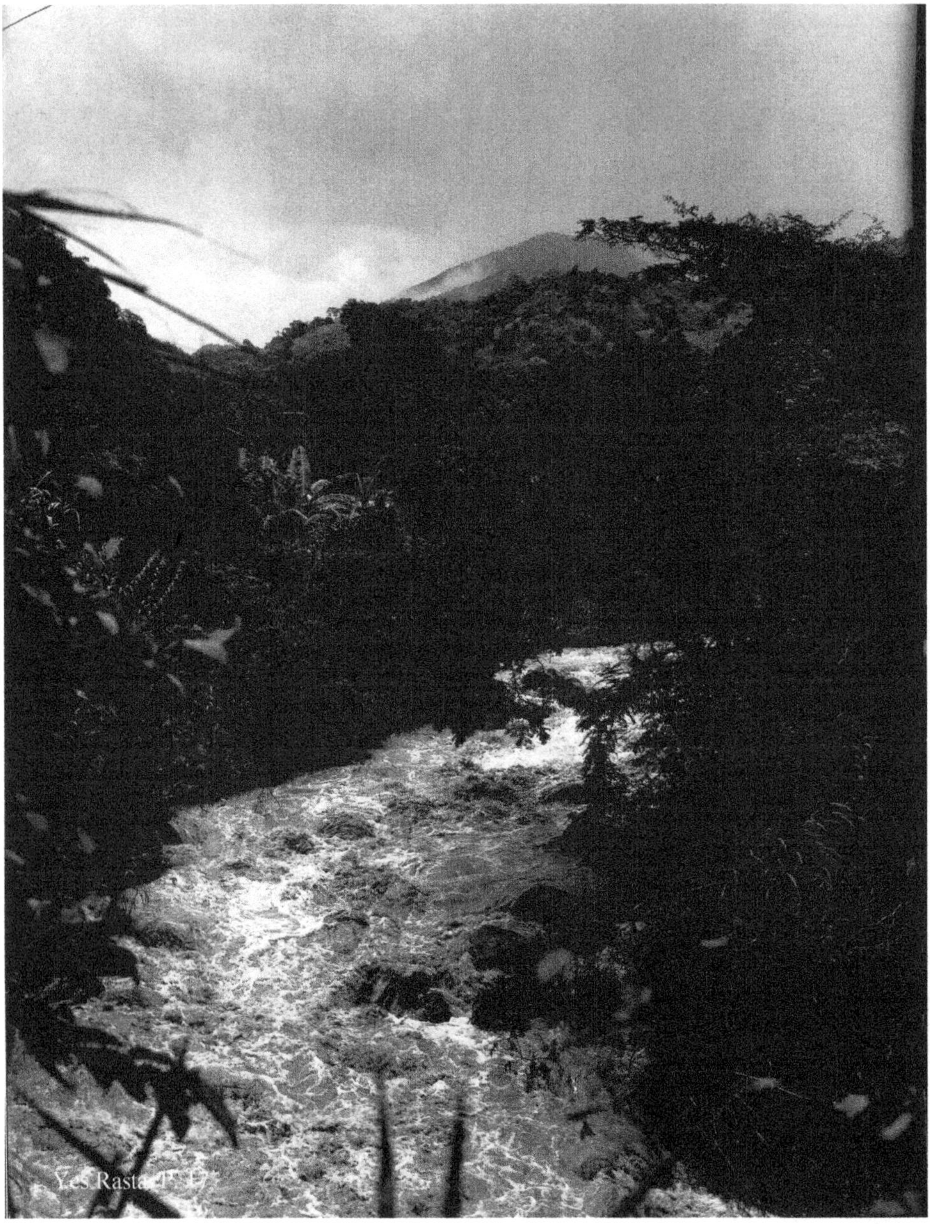
Yes Rasta

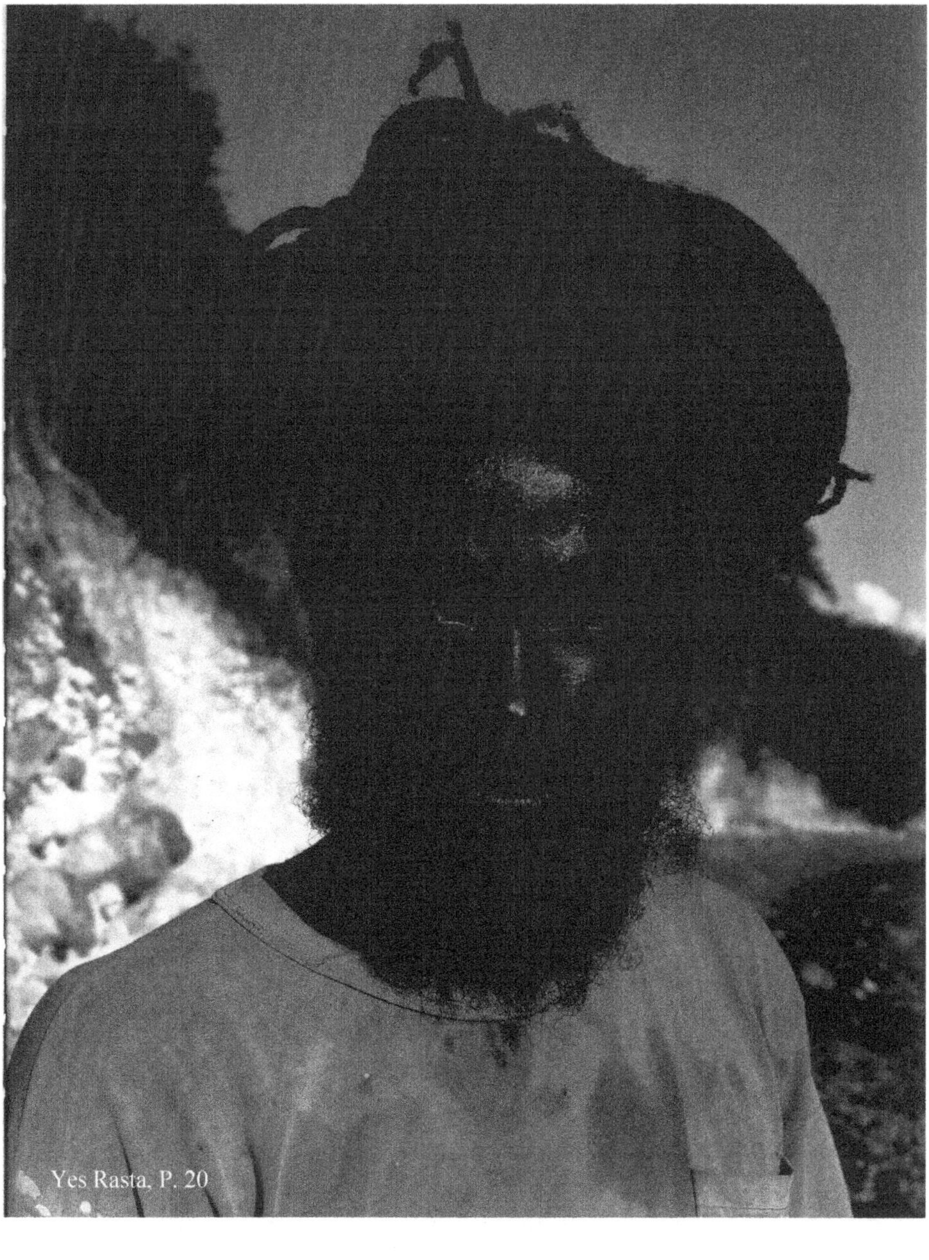

Yes Rasta, P. 20

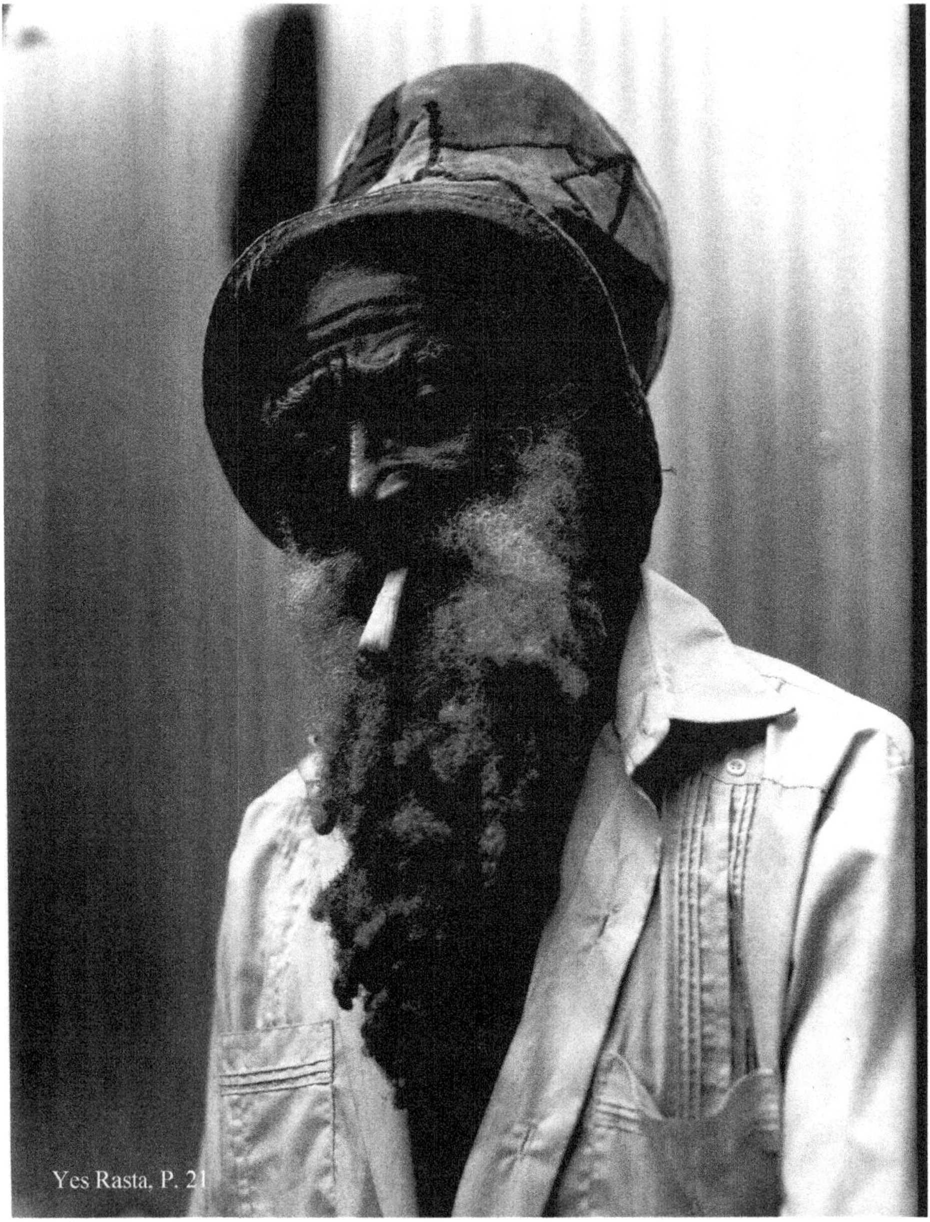

Yes Rasta, P. 21

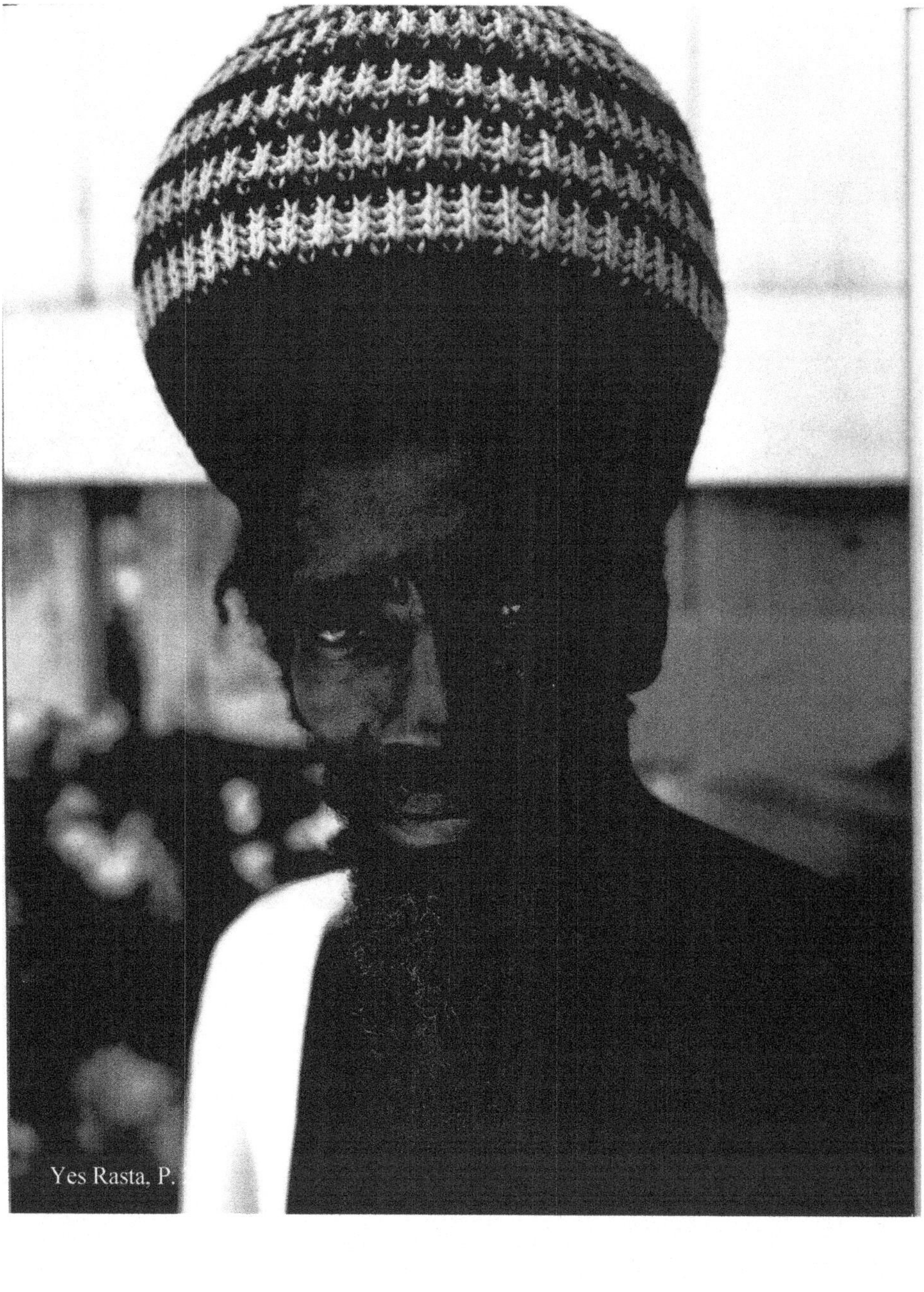
Yes Rasta, P.

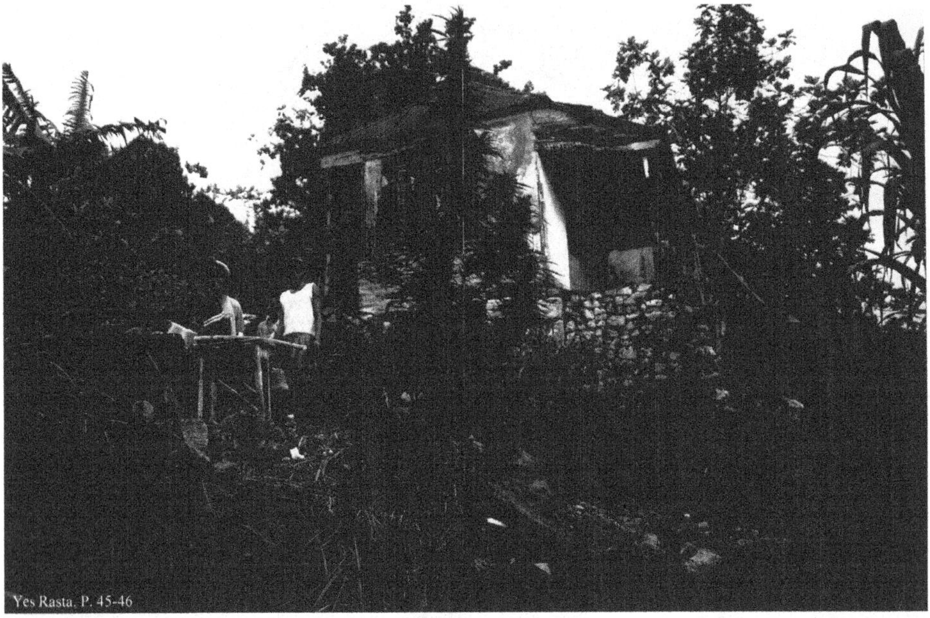
Yes Rasta. P. 45-46

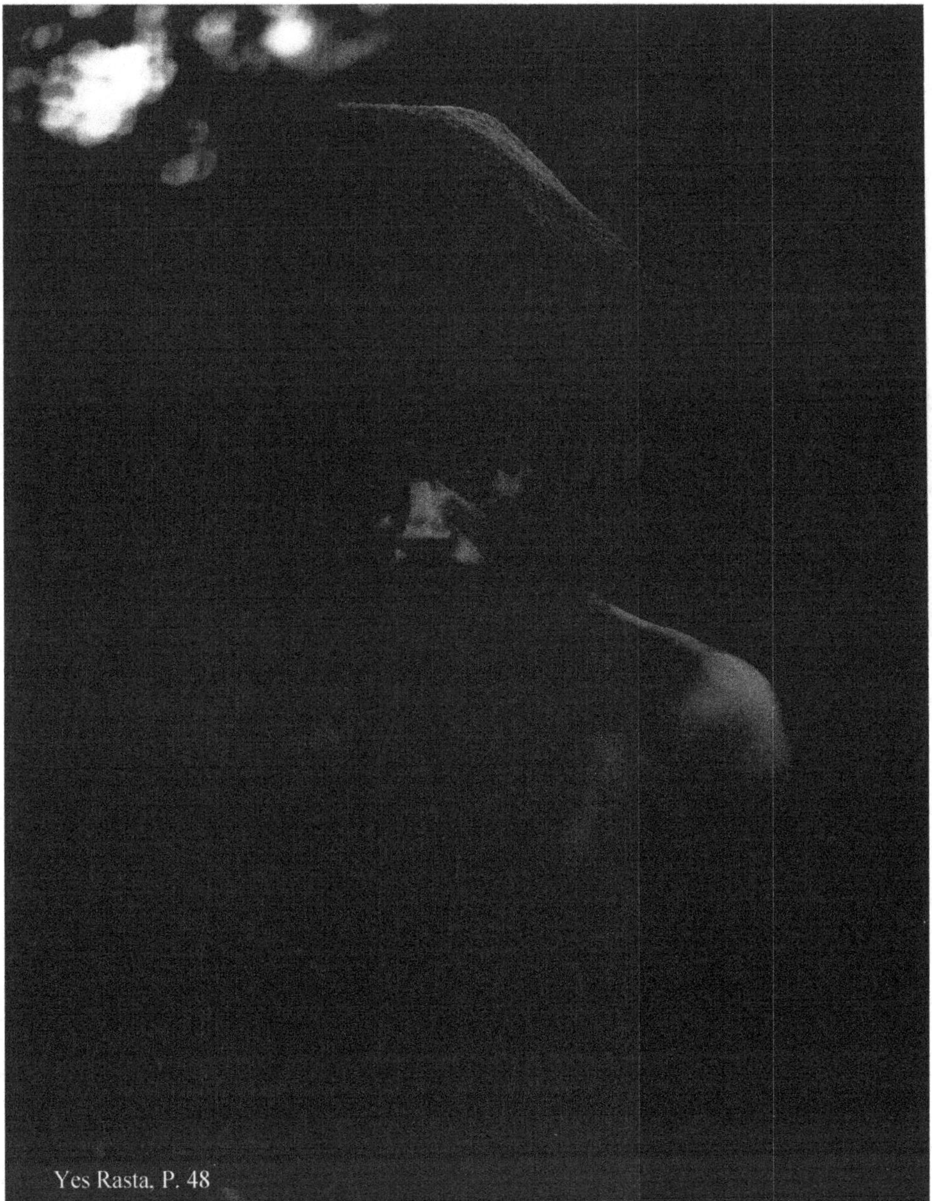

Yes Rasta, P. 48

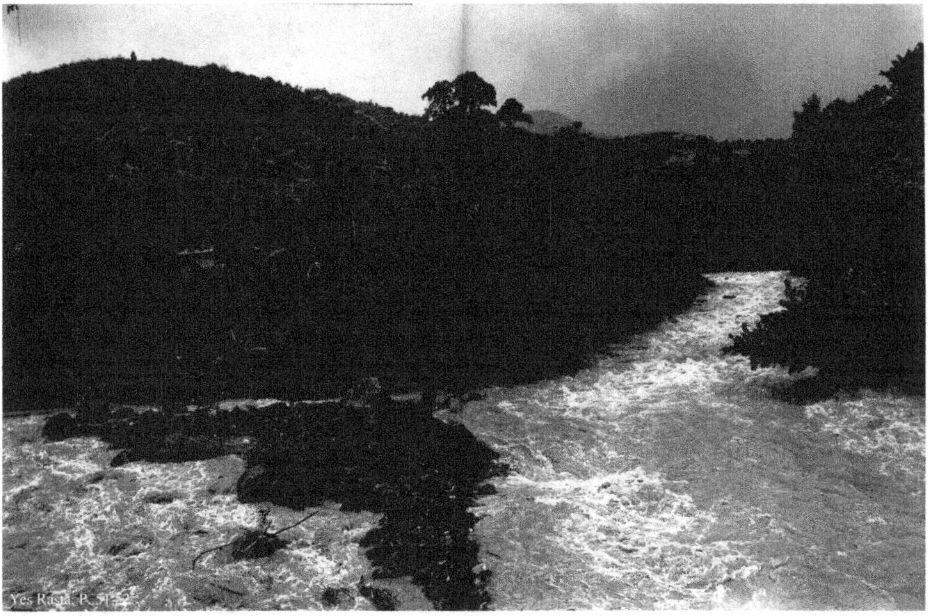

Yes Rasta. P. 51-52

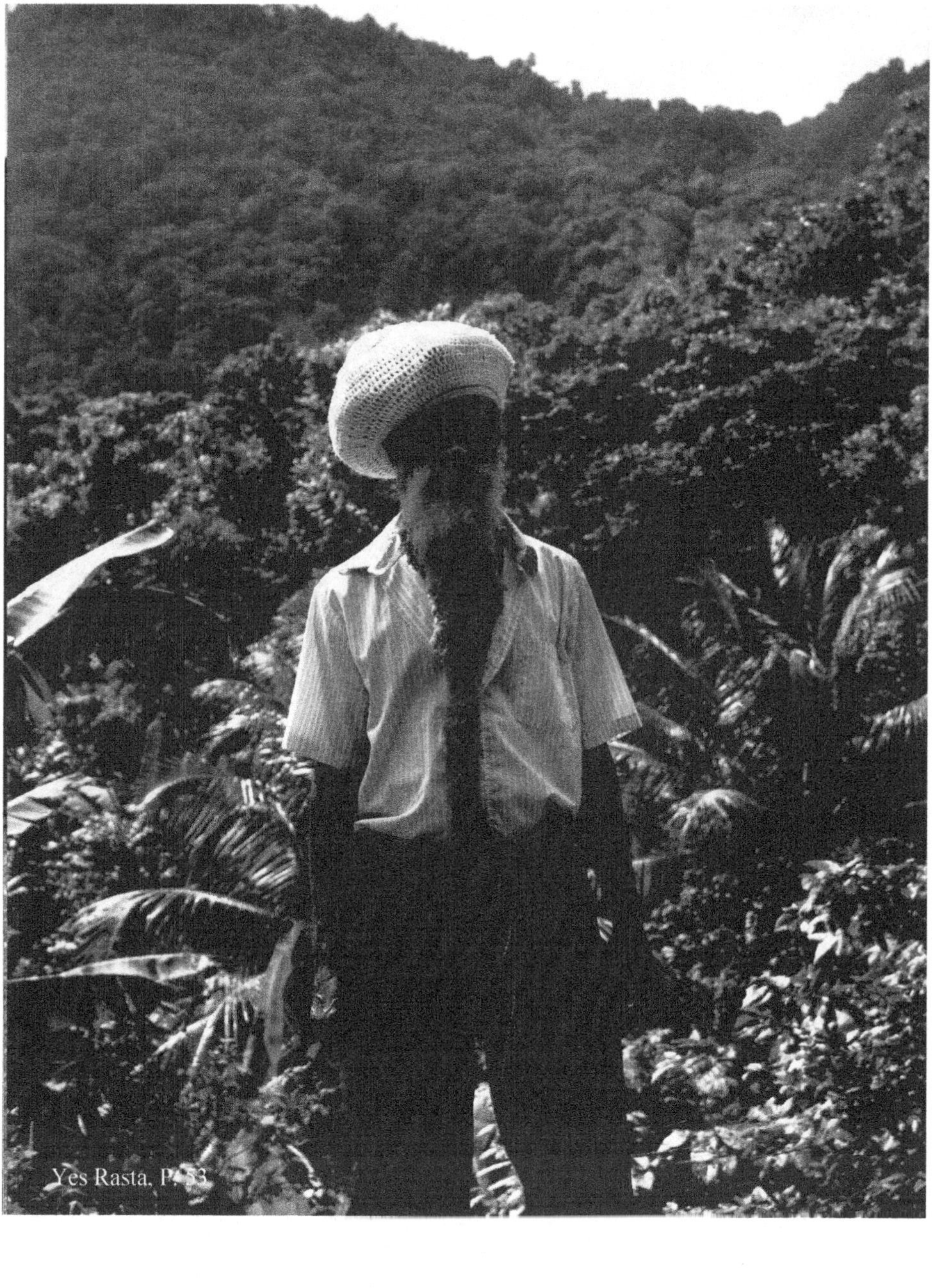

Yes Rasta, P. 53

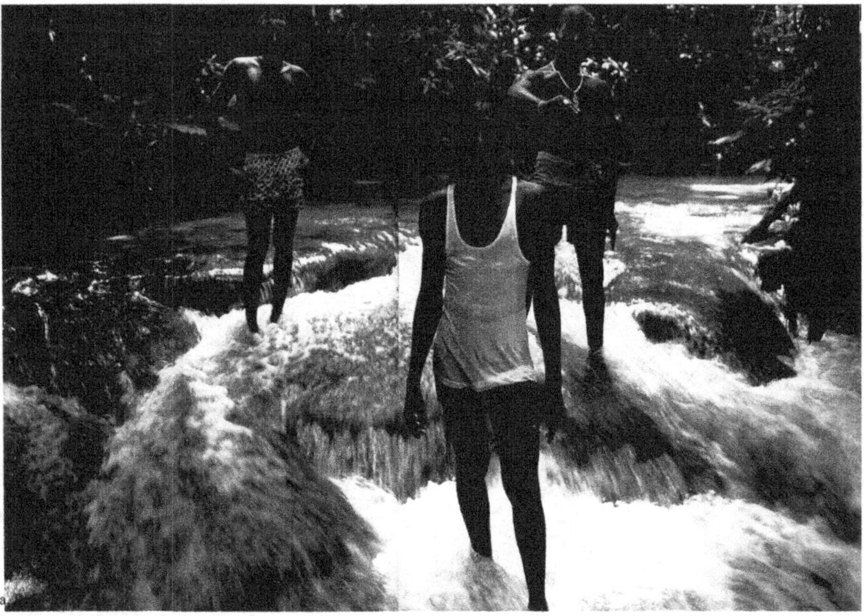

Yes Rasta

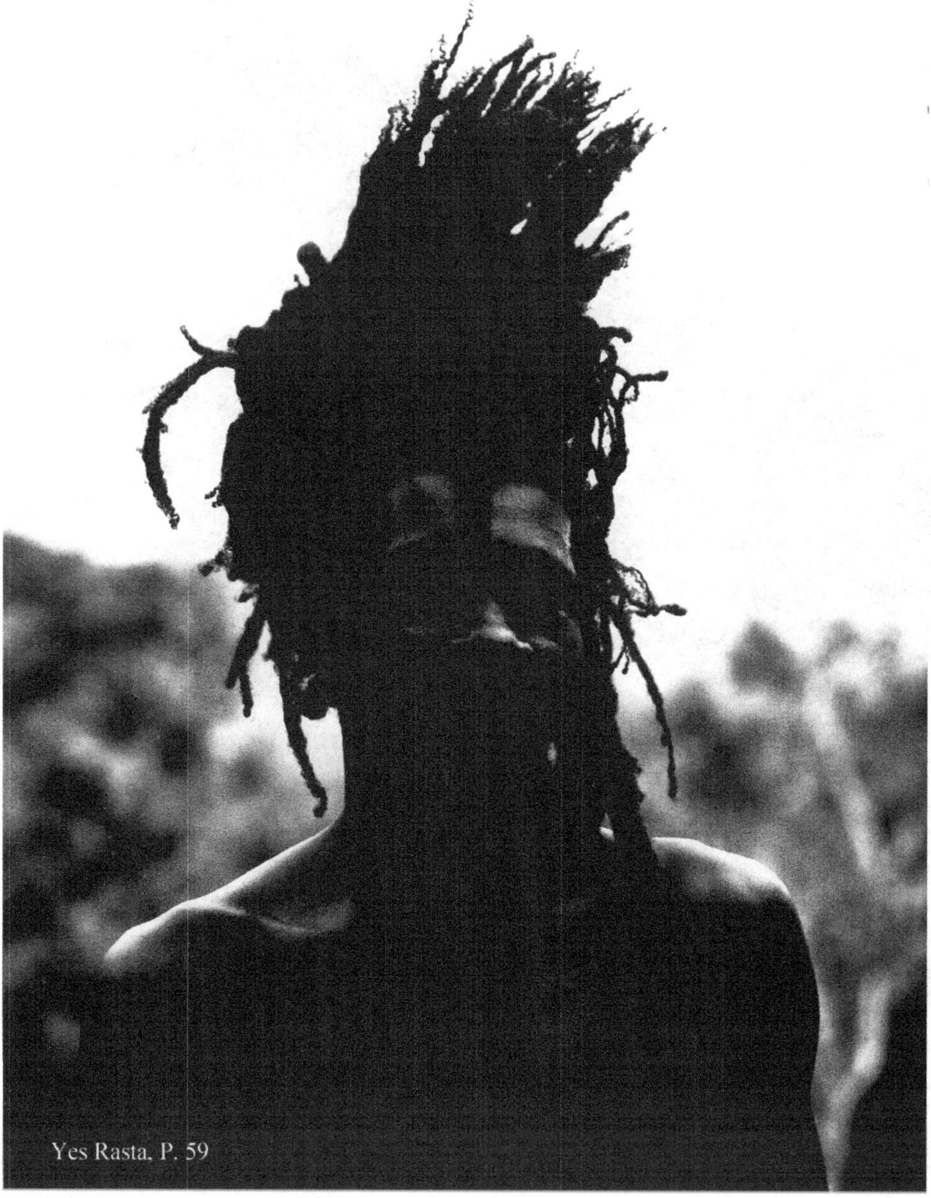
Yes Rasta, P. 59

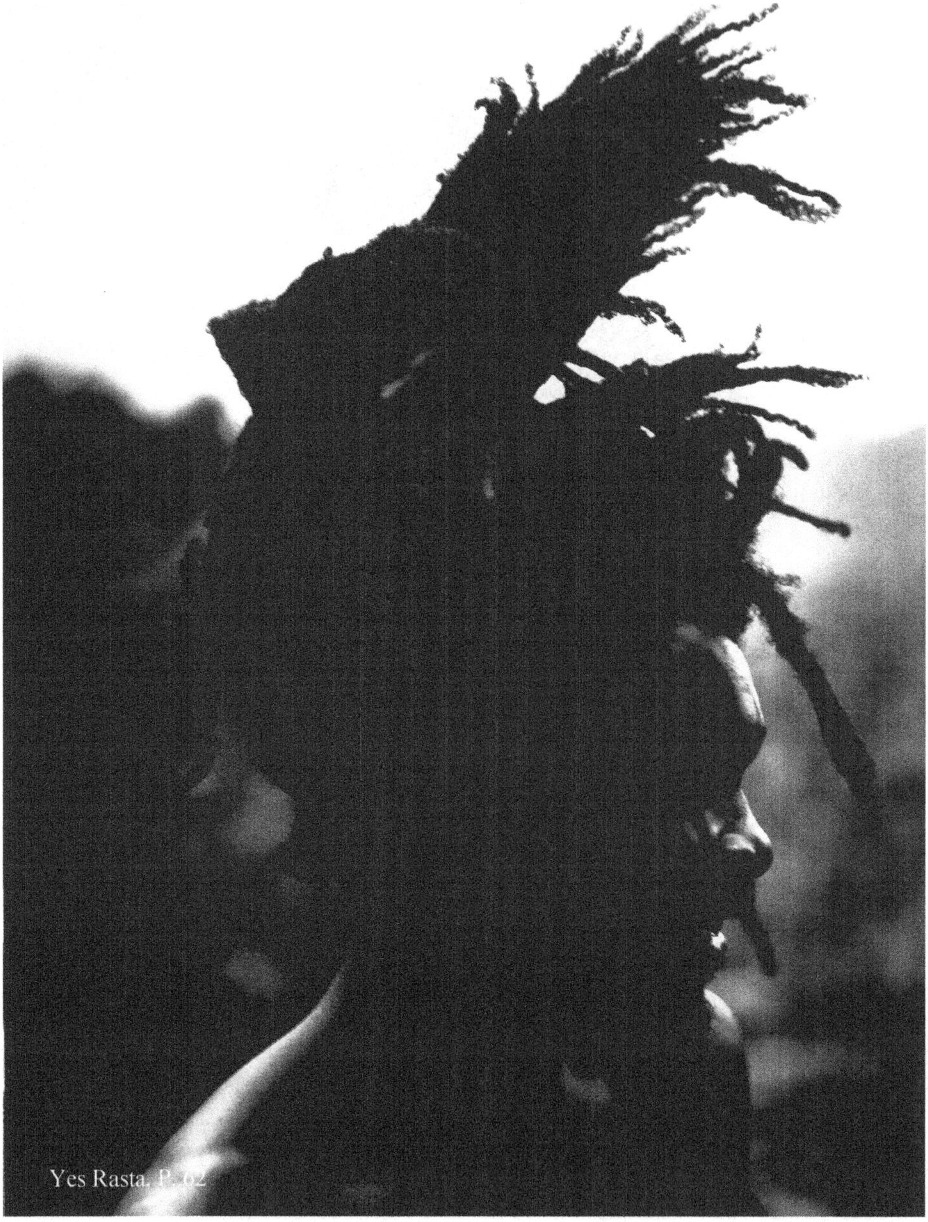
Yes Rasta, P. 62

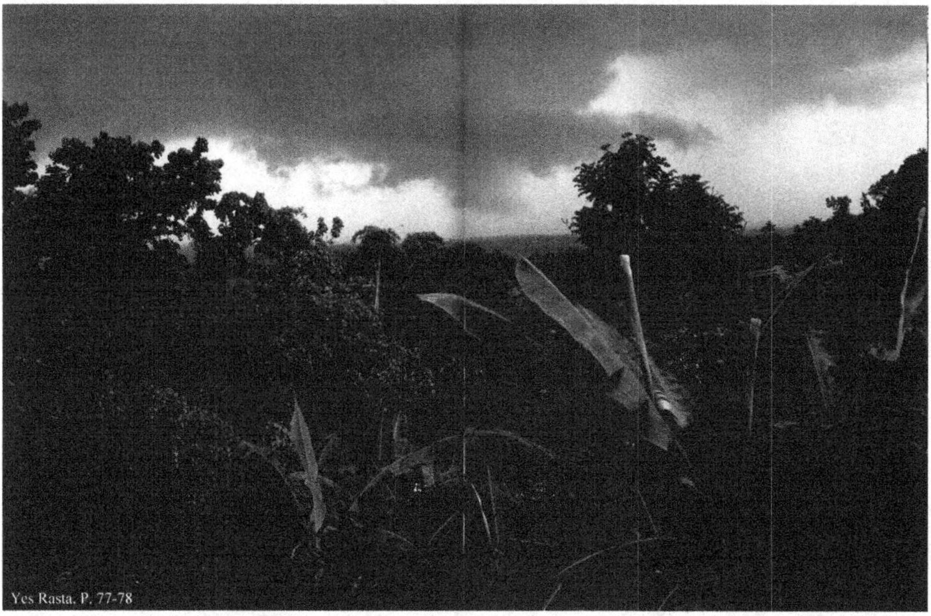

Yes Rasta. P. 77-78

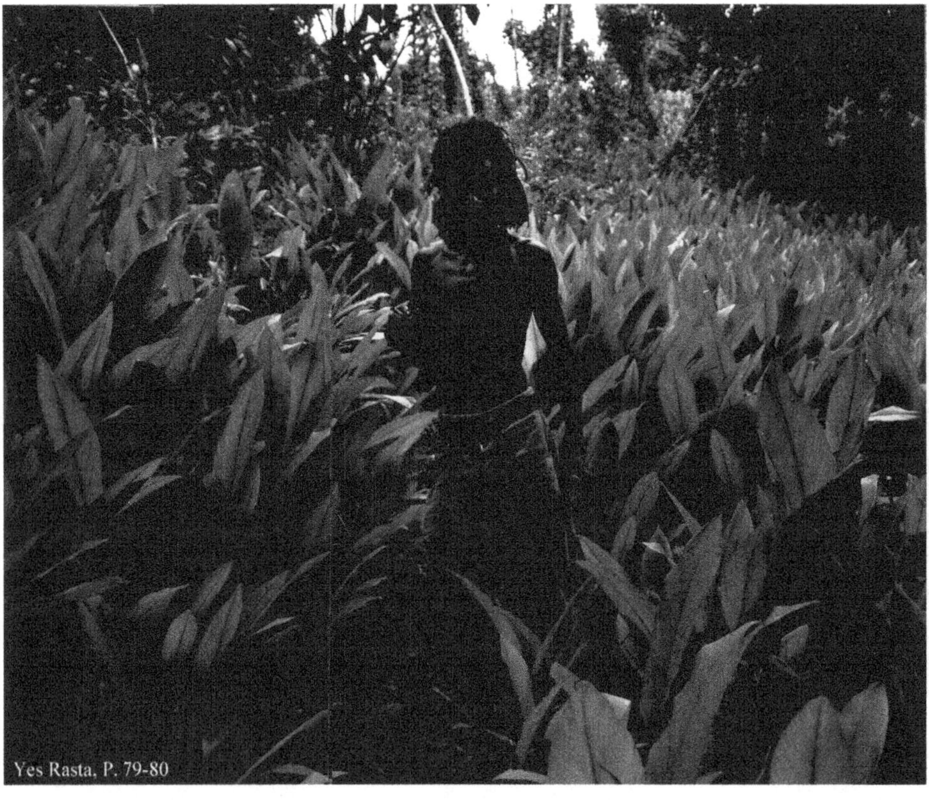
Yes Rasta, P. 79-80

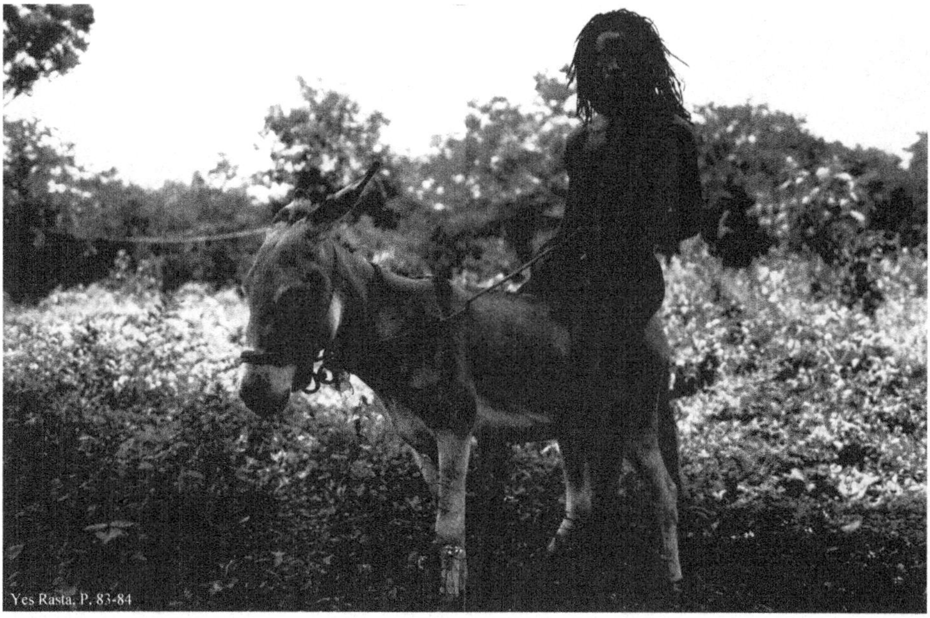

Yes Rasta, P. 83-84

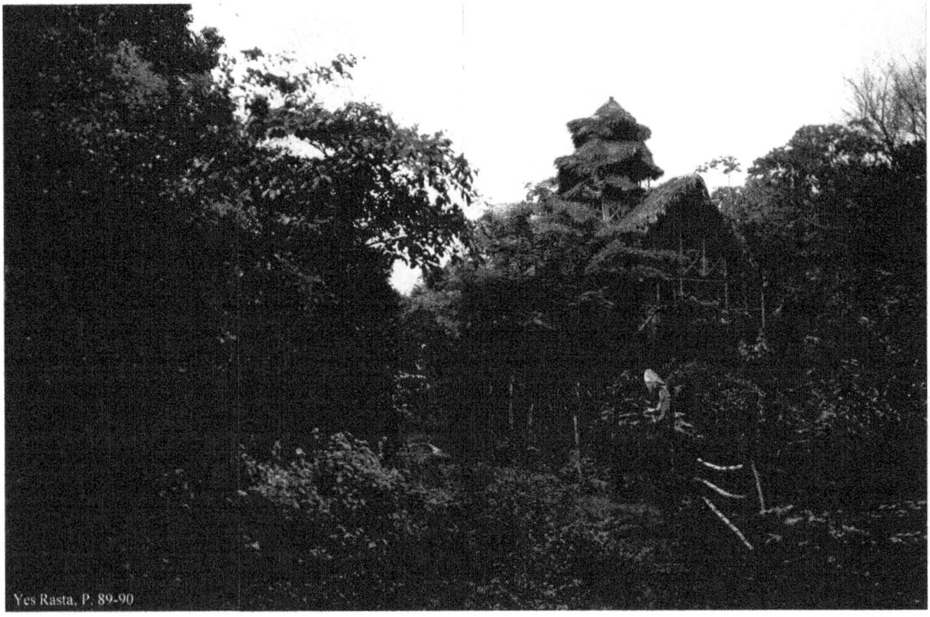

Yes Rasta, P. 89-90

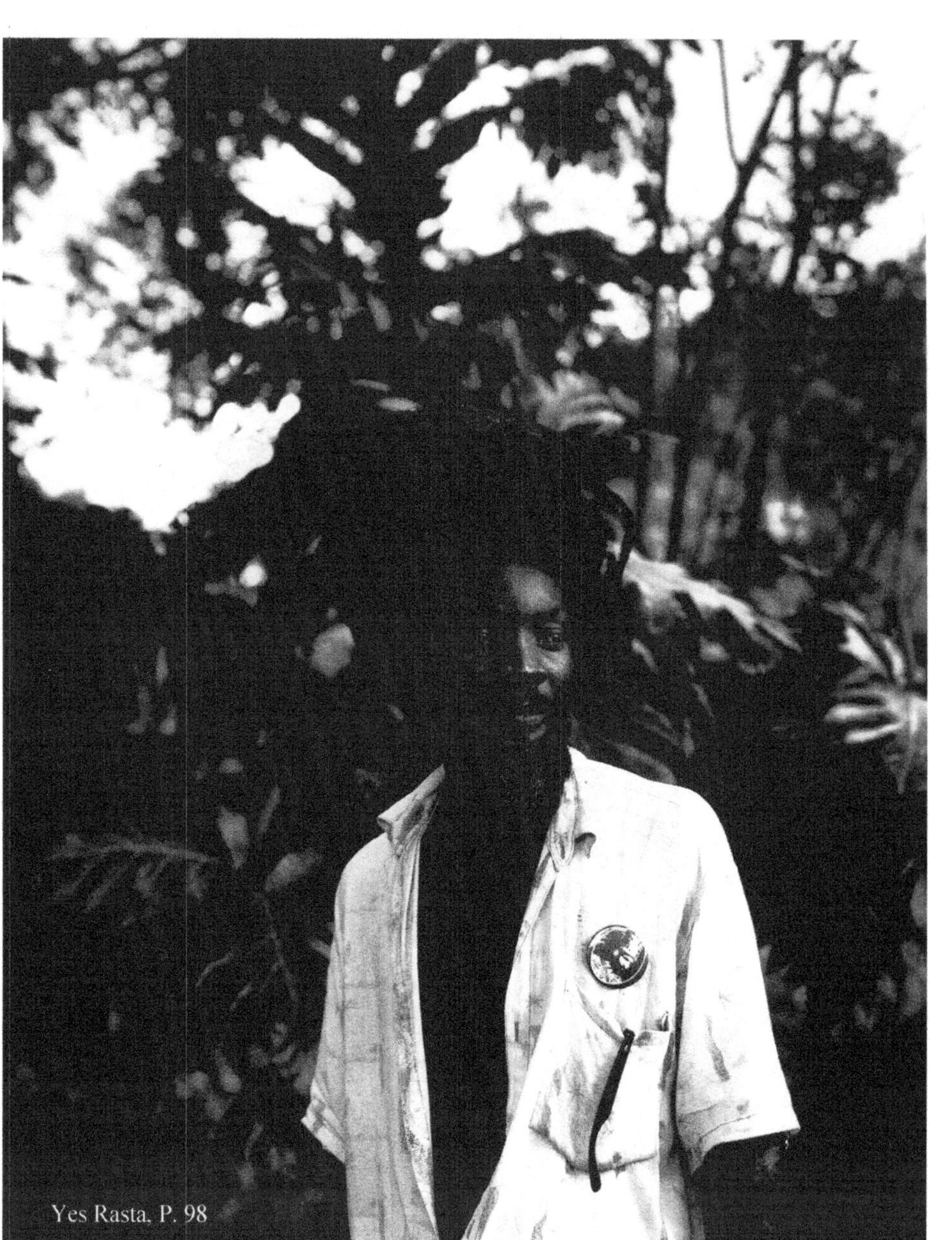

Yes Rasta, P. 98

Yes Rasta, P. 101-102

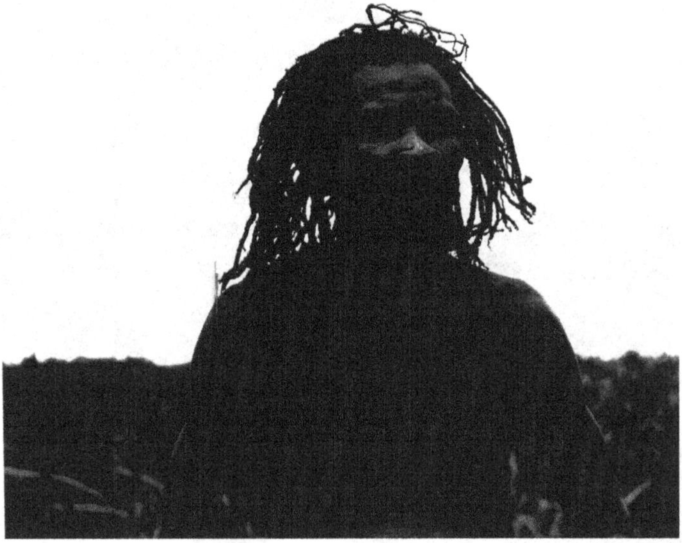

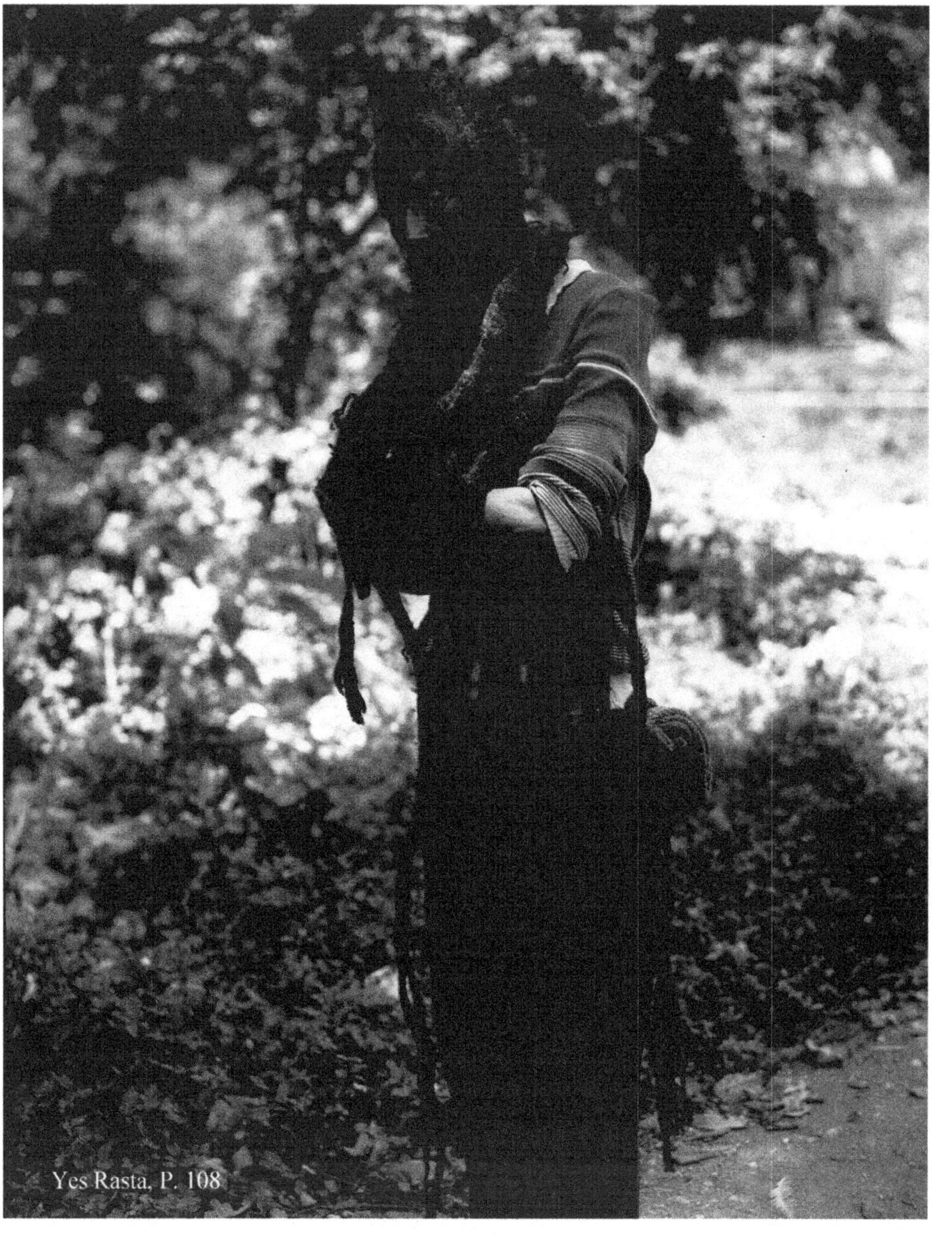
Yes Rasta, P. 108

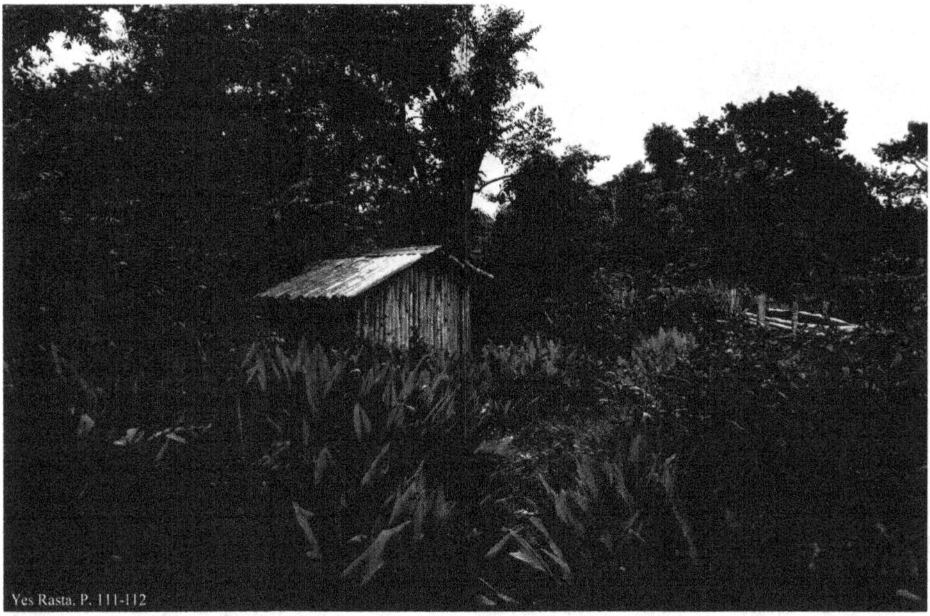

Yes Rasta. P. 111-112

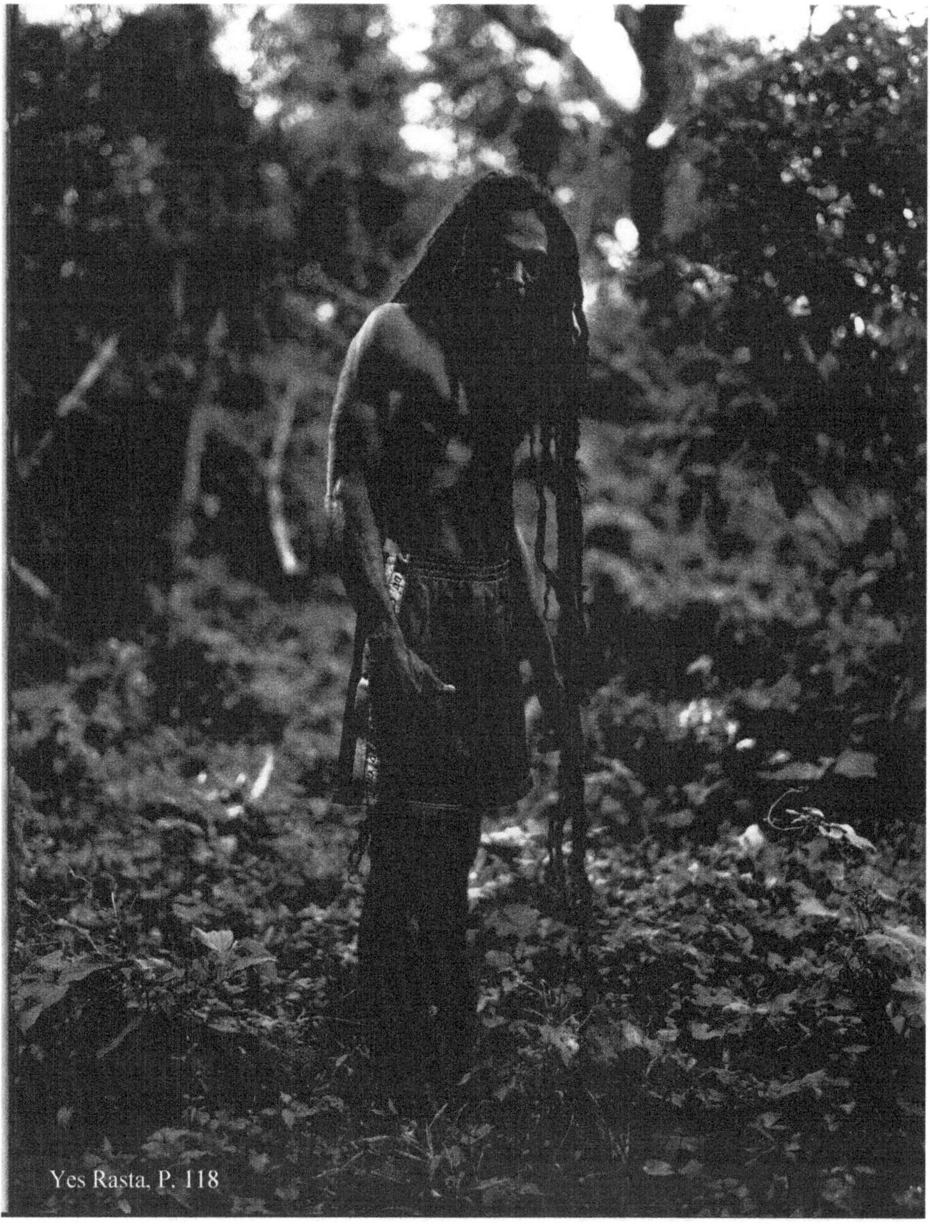

Yes Rasta, P. 118

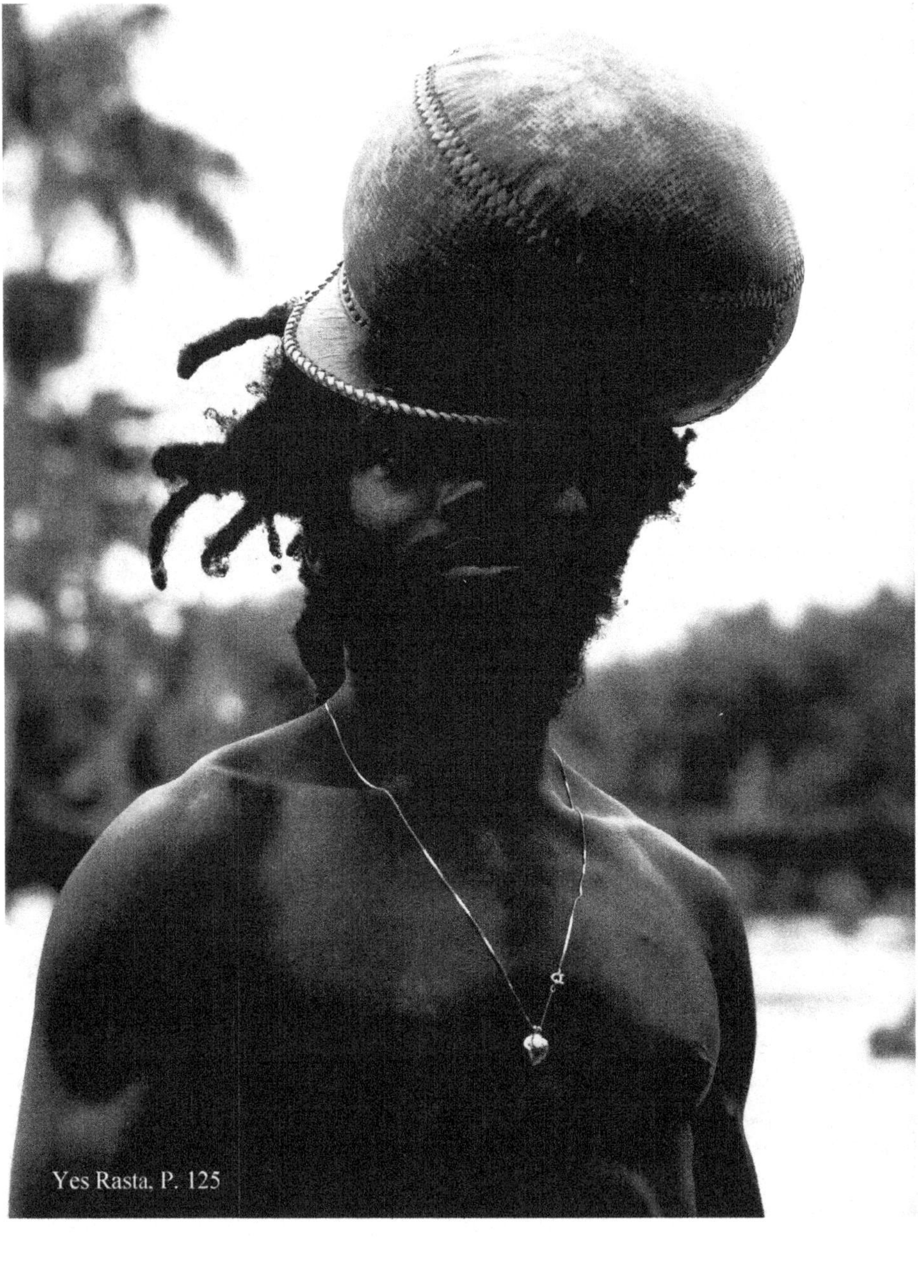

Yes Rasta, P. 125

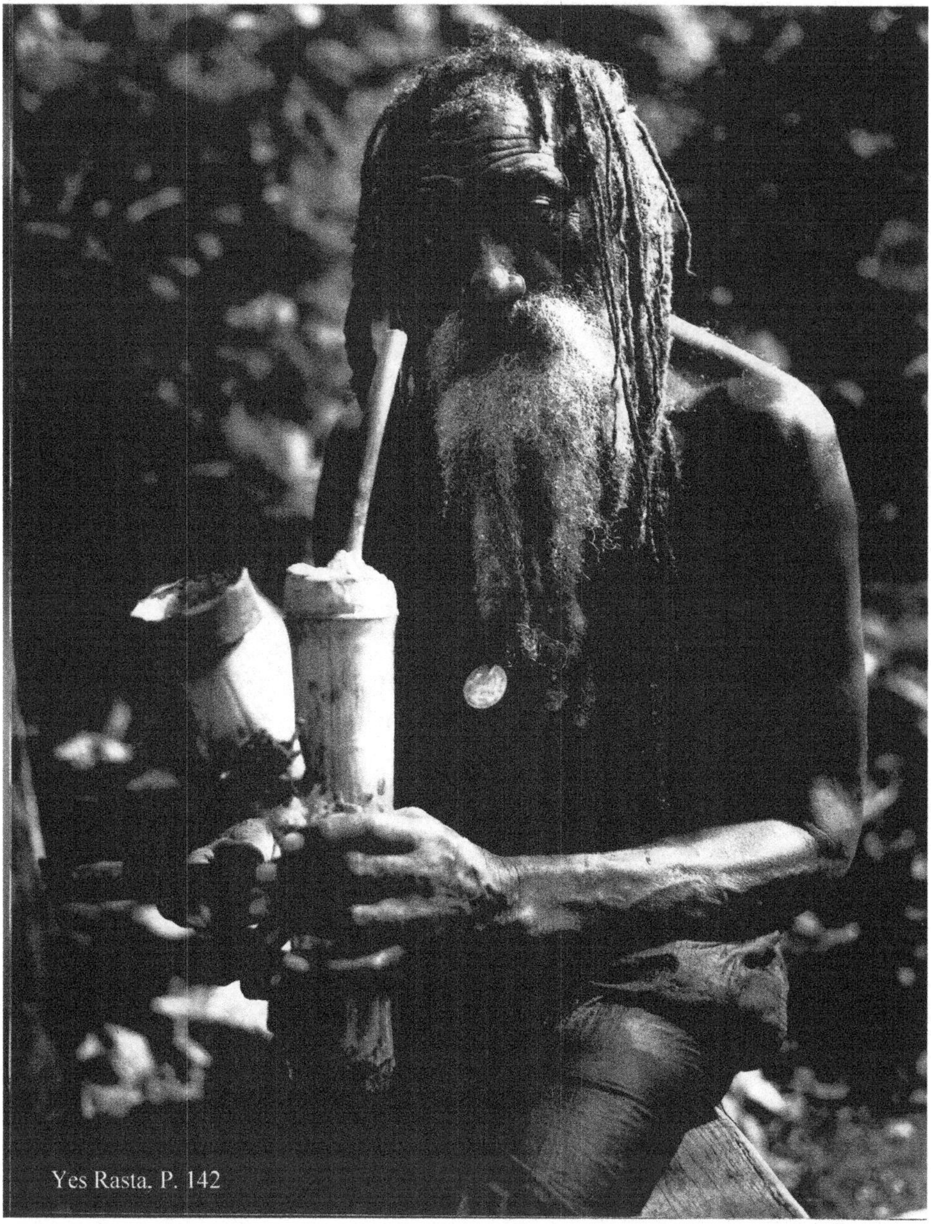
Yes Rasta, P. 142

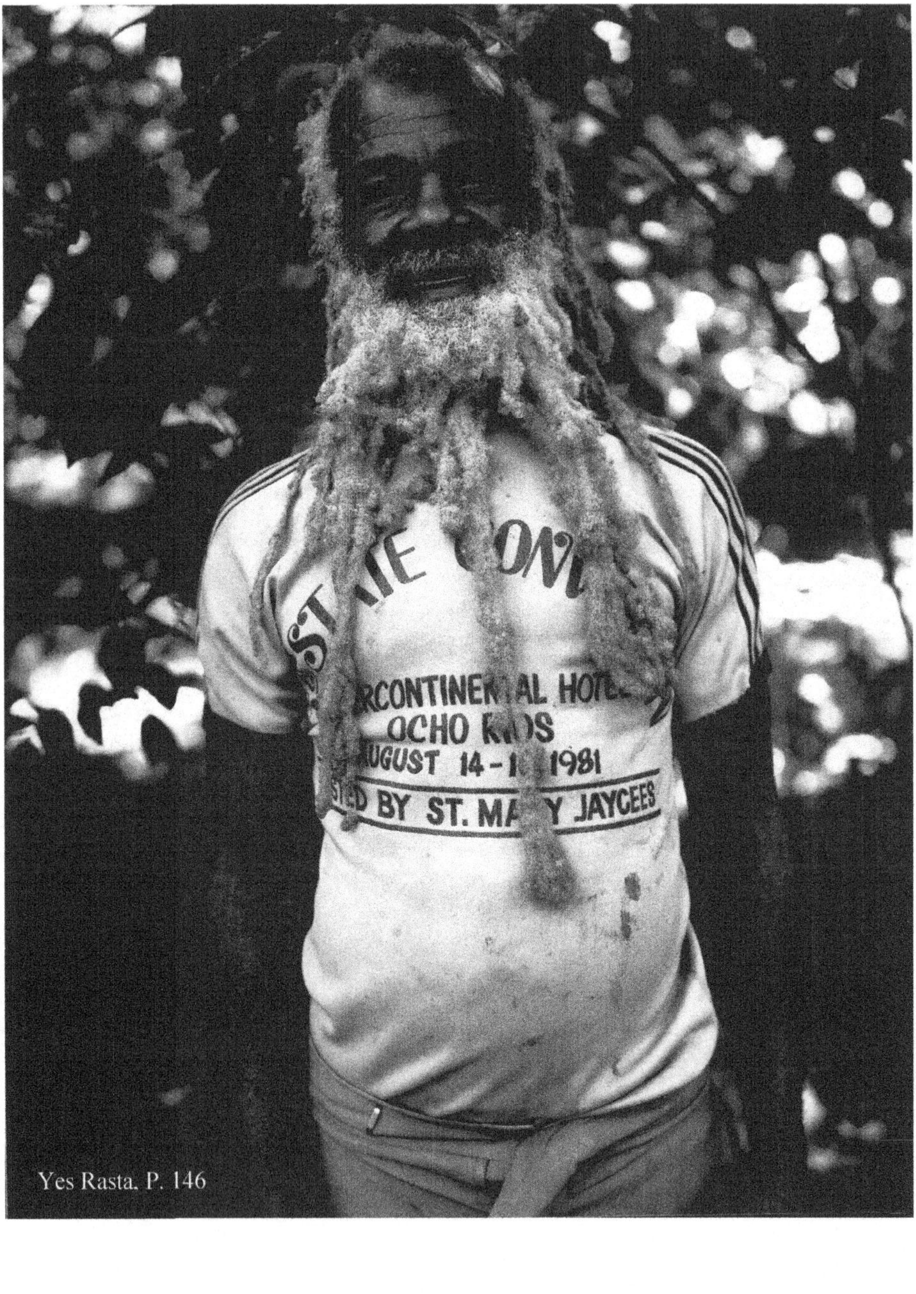

Yes Rasta. P. 146

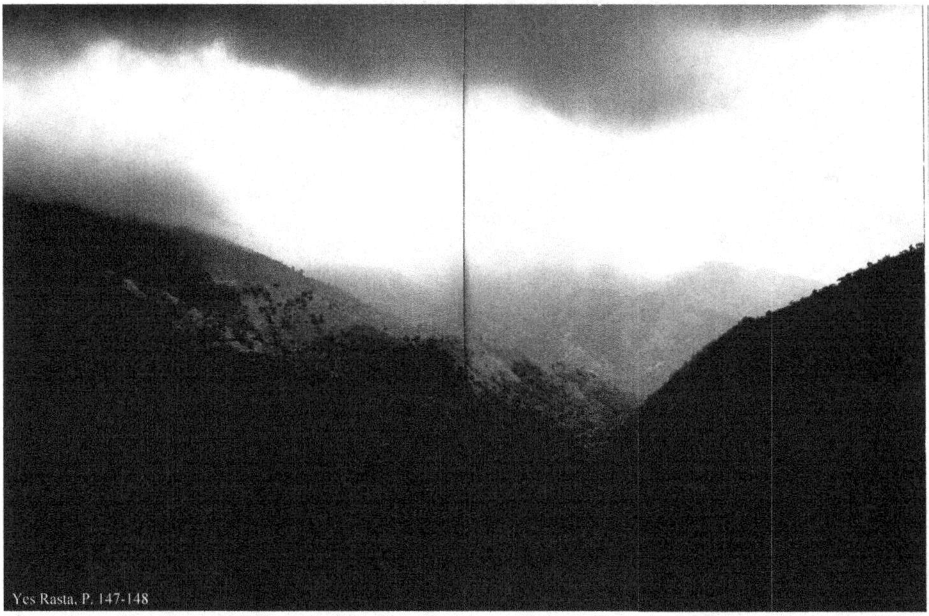

Yes Rasta, P. 147-148

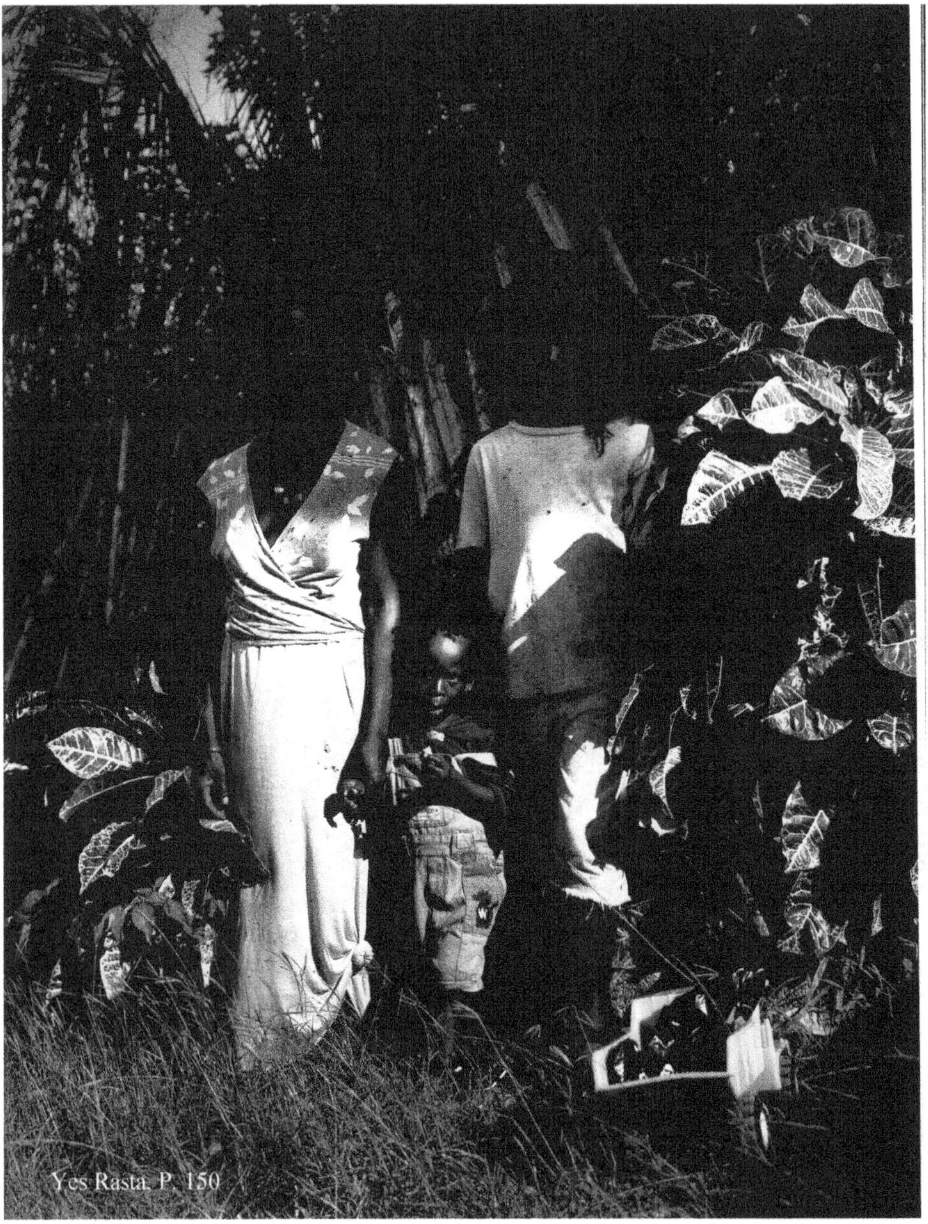
Yes Rasta, P. 150

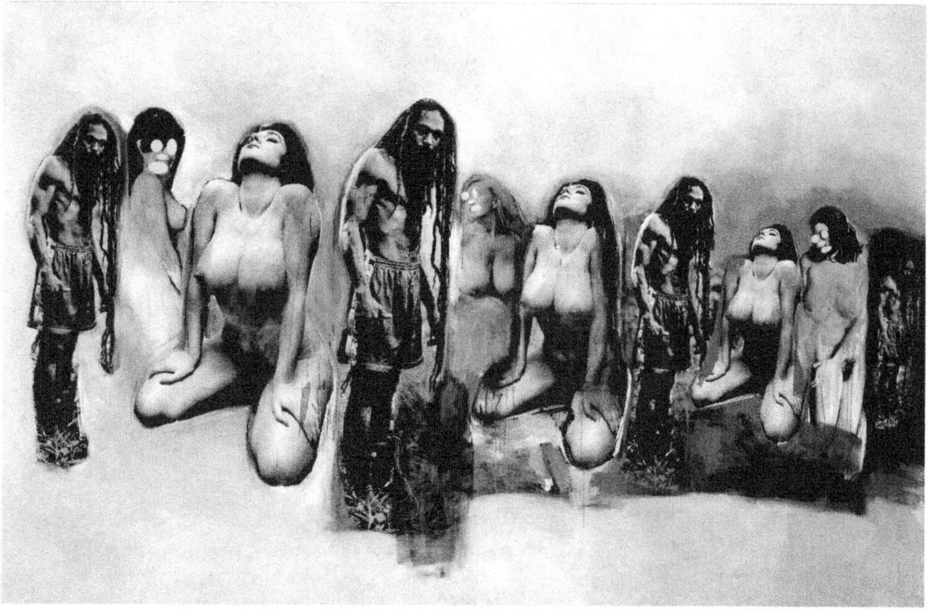

R

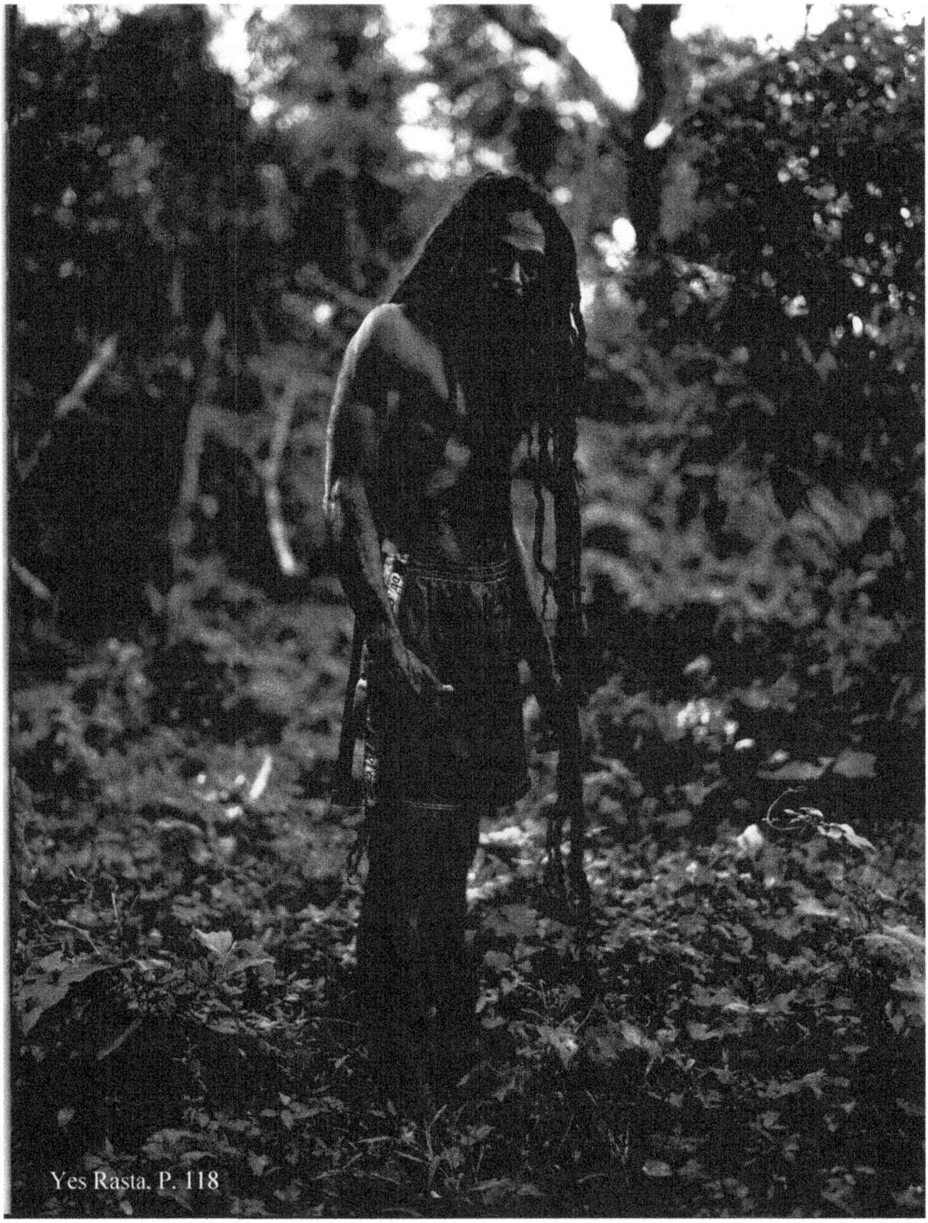

Yes Rasta. P. 118

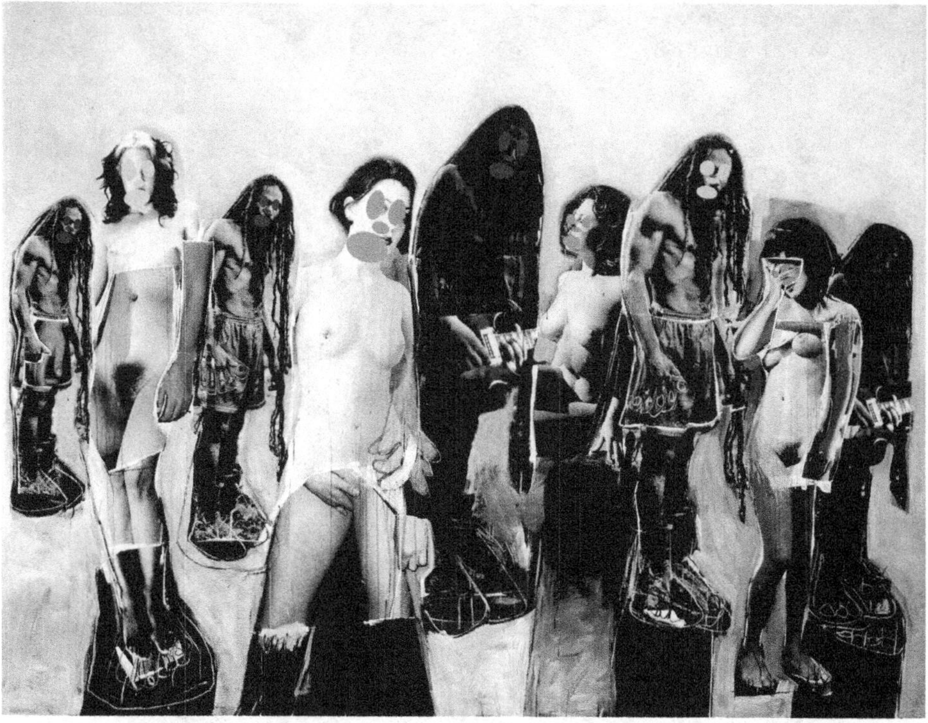

S

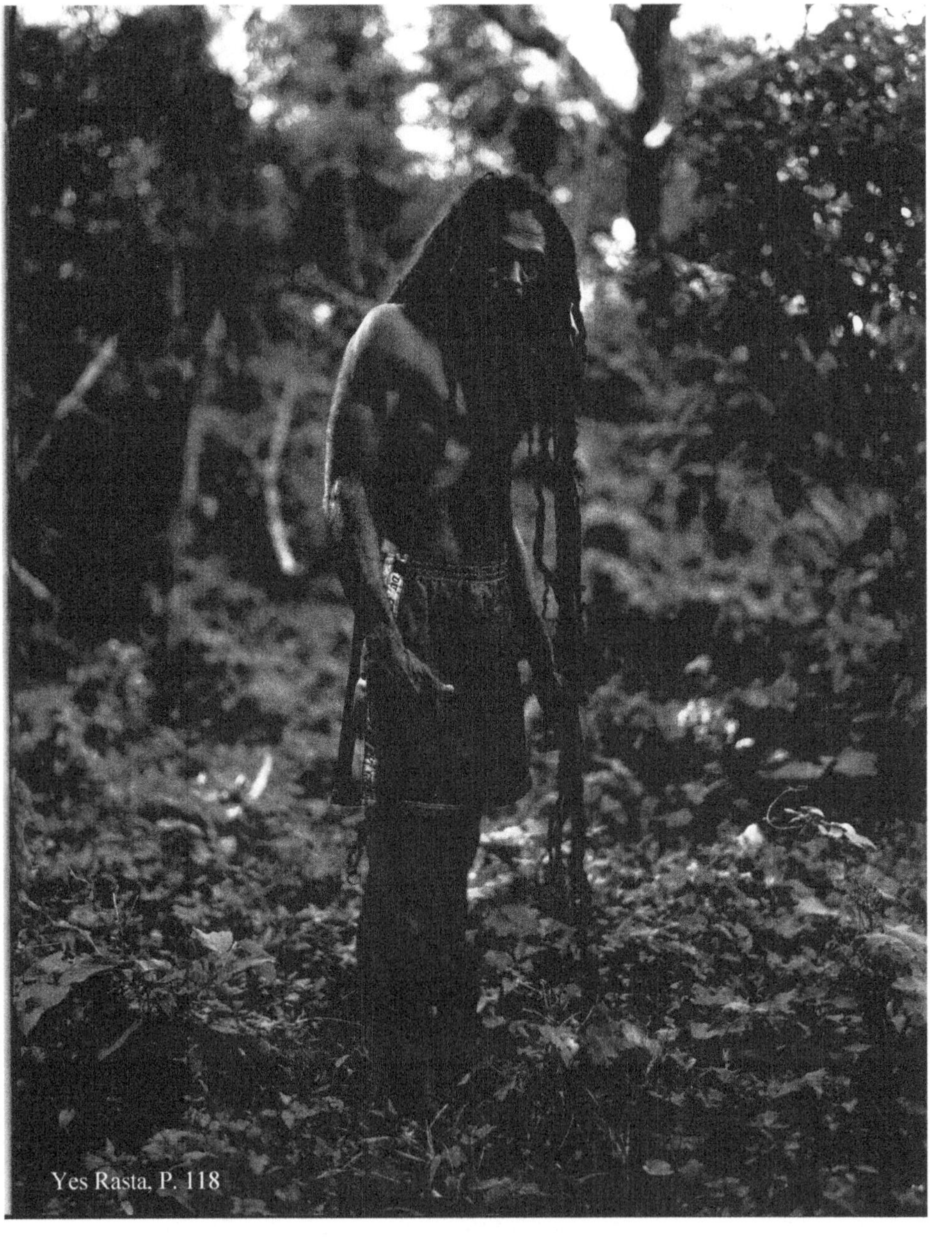

Yes Rasta, P. 118

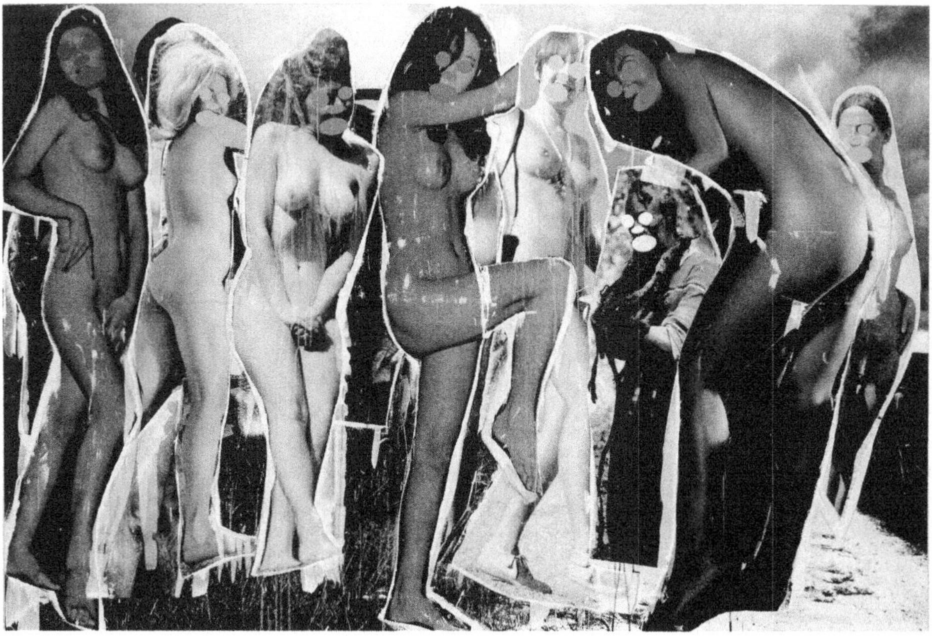

T

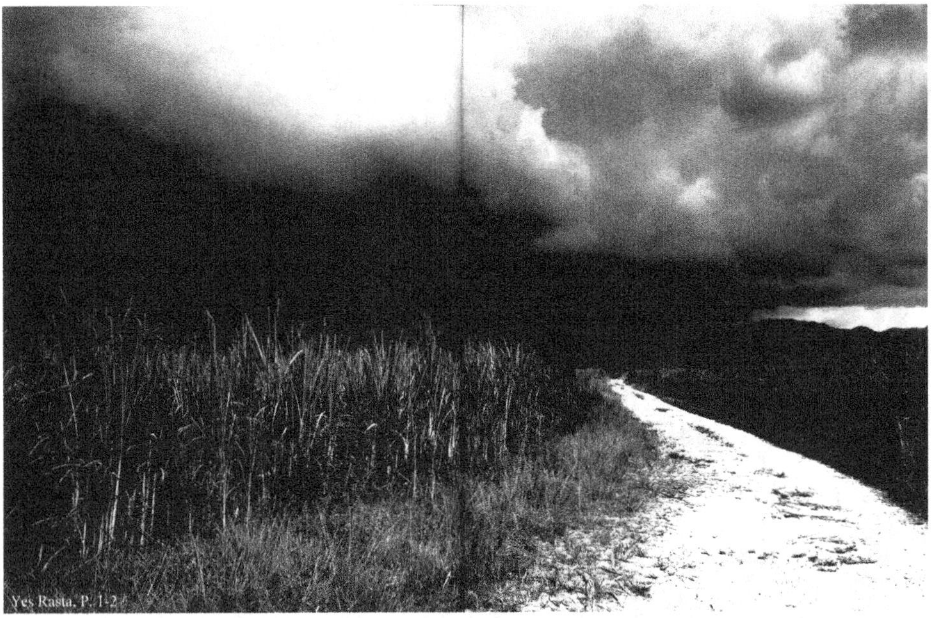
Yes Rasta, P. 1-2

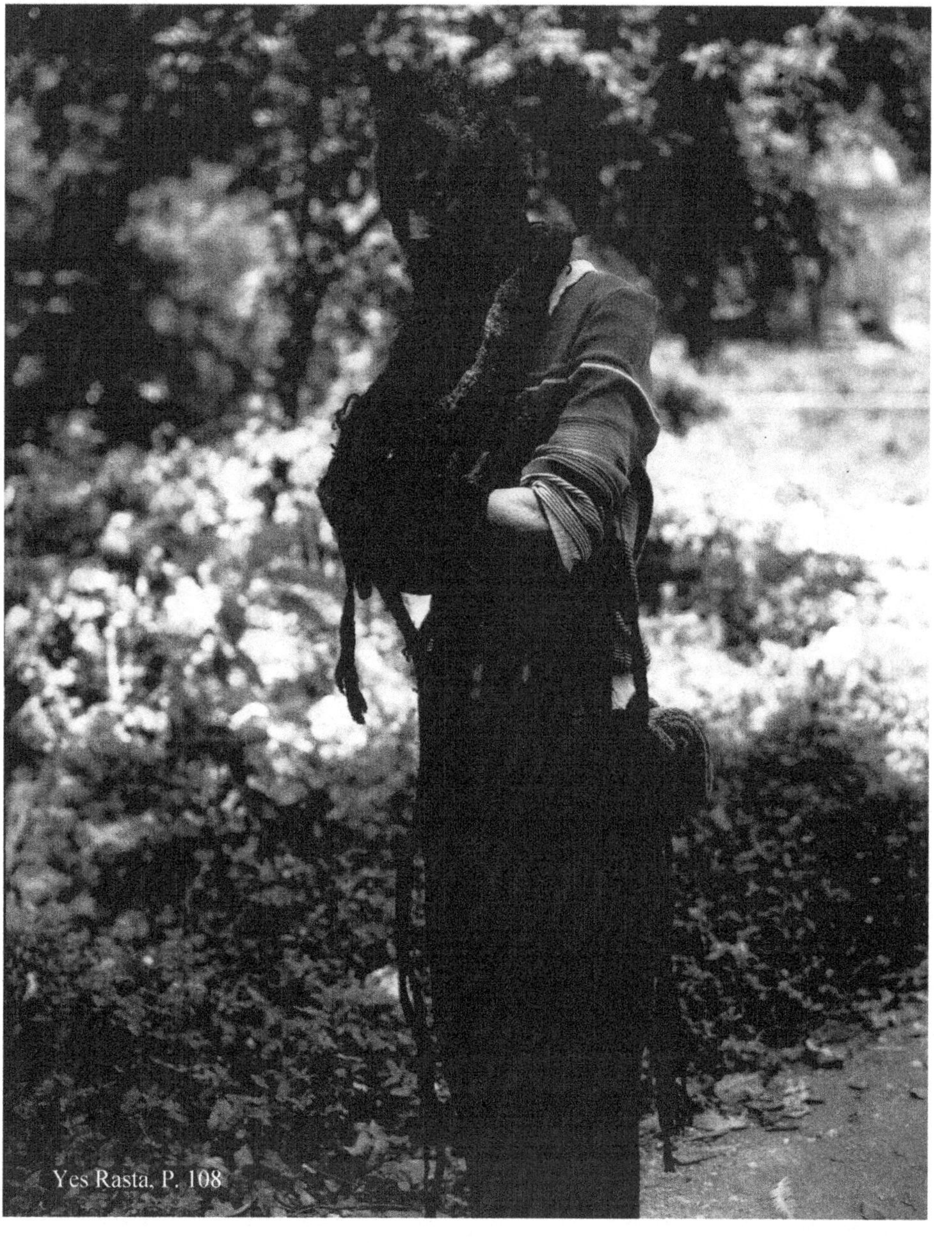

Yes Rasta, P. 108

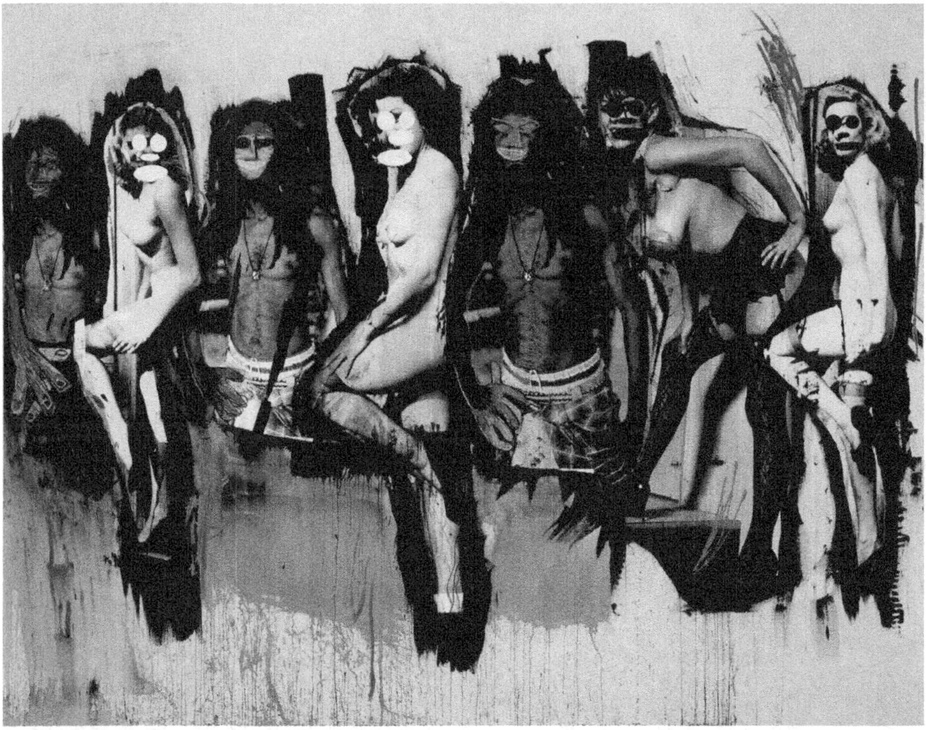

U

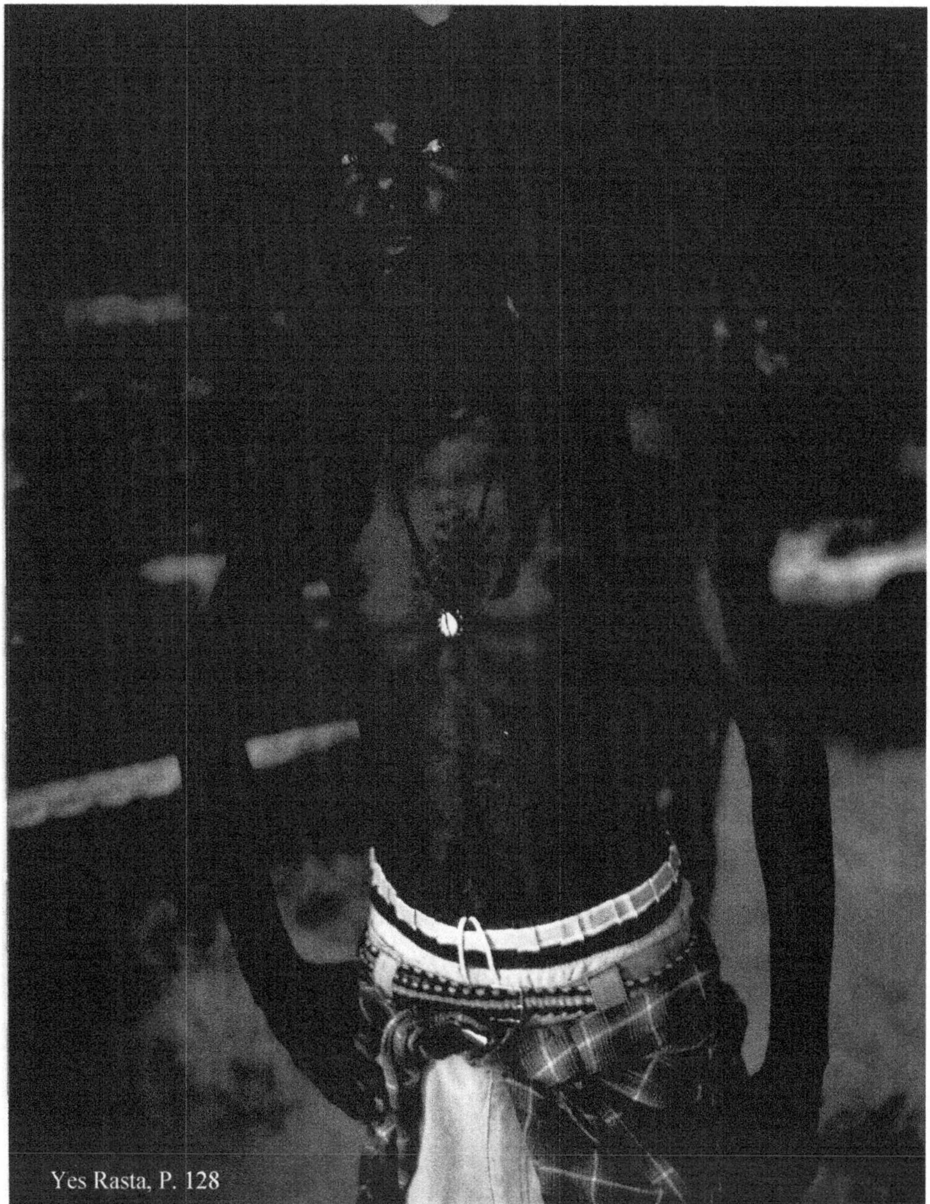

Yes Rasta, P. 128

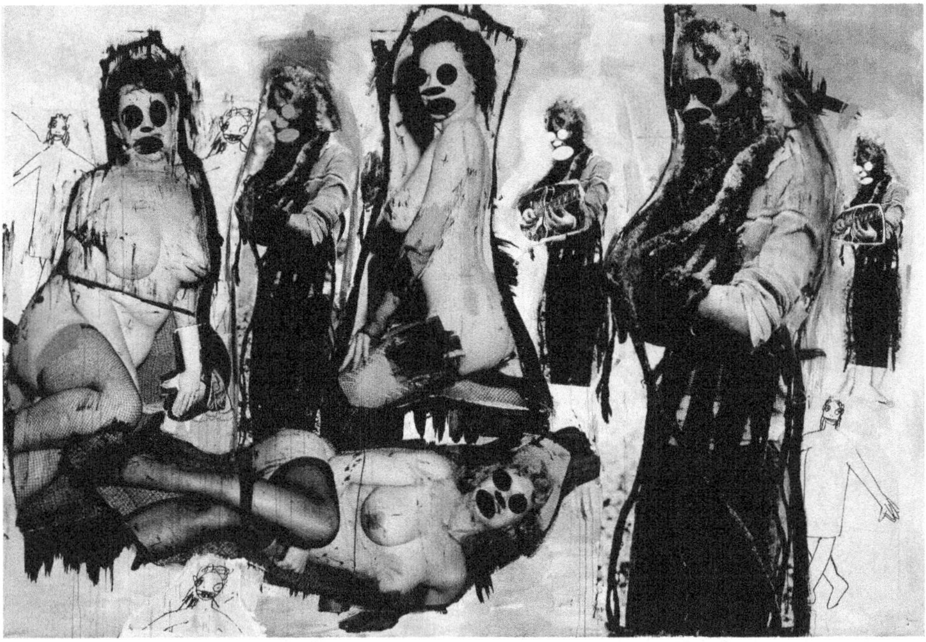

V

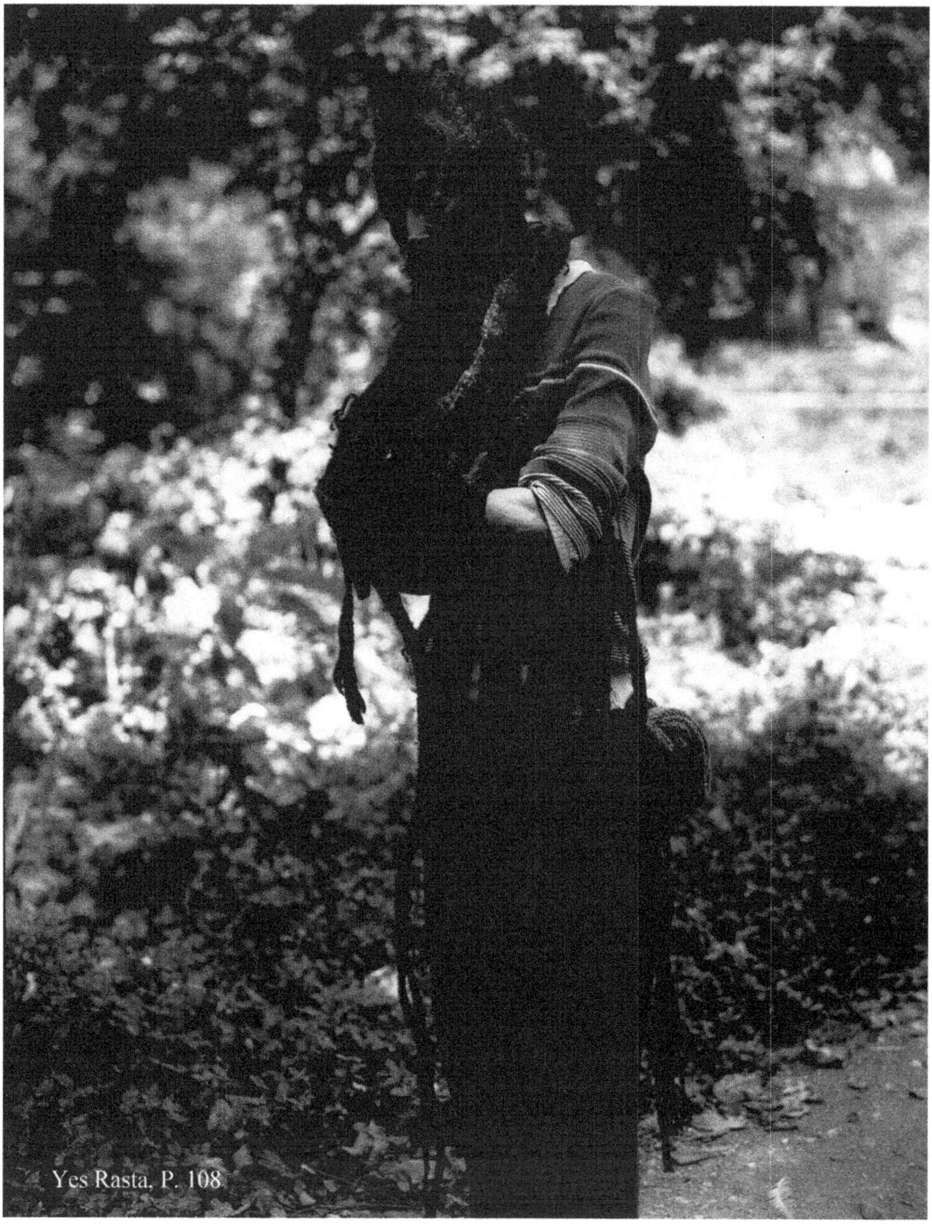
Yes Rasta, P. 108

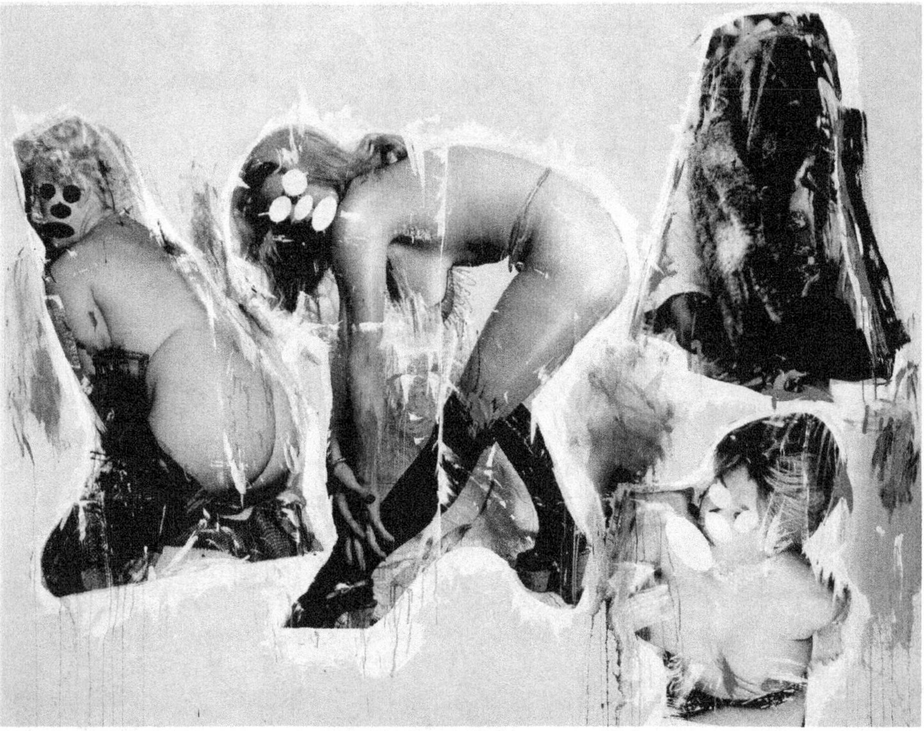

W

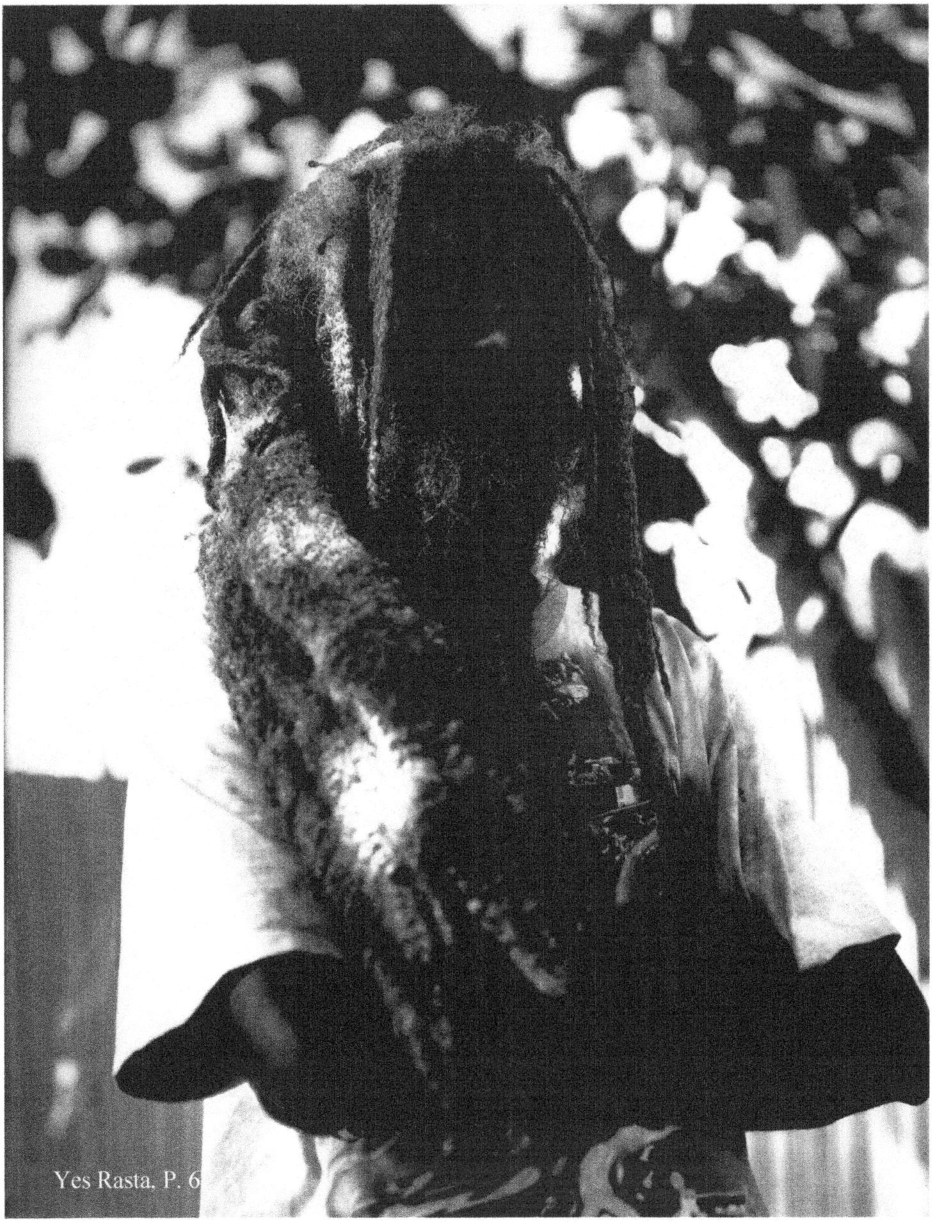

Yes Rasta, P. 6

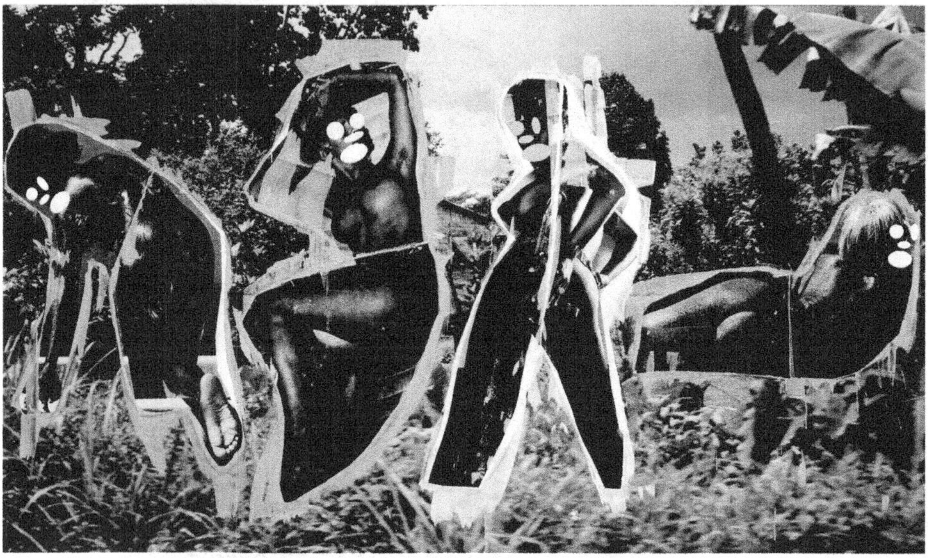

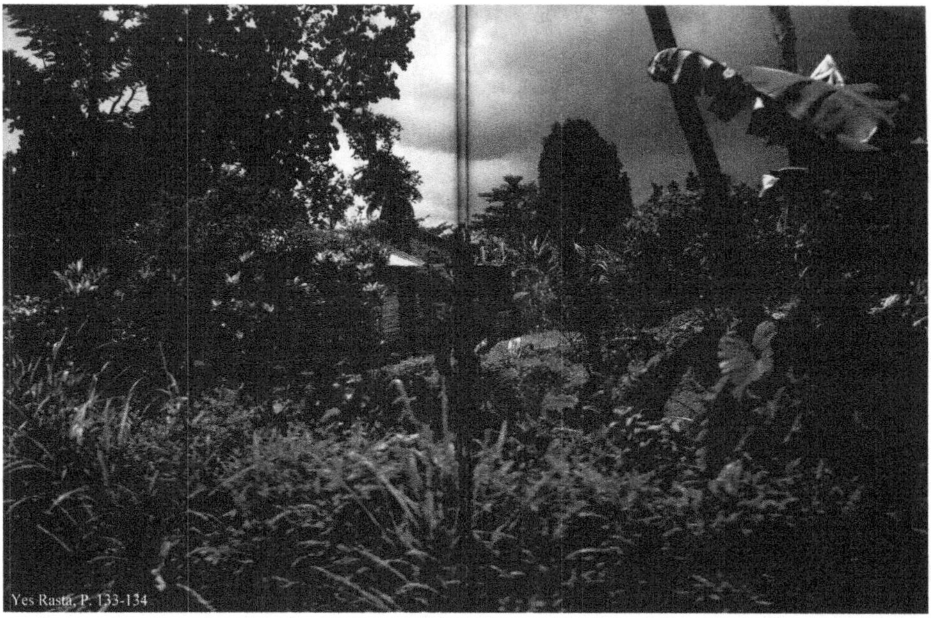

Yes Rasta, P. 133-134

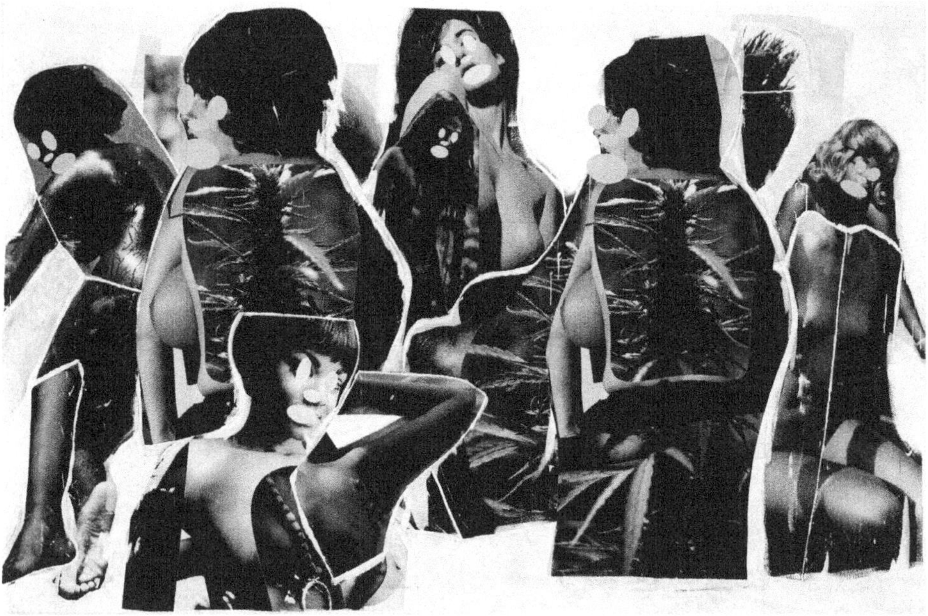

Y

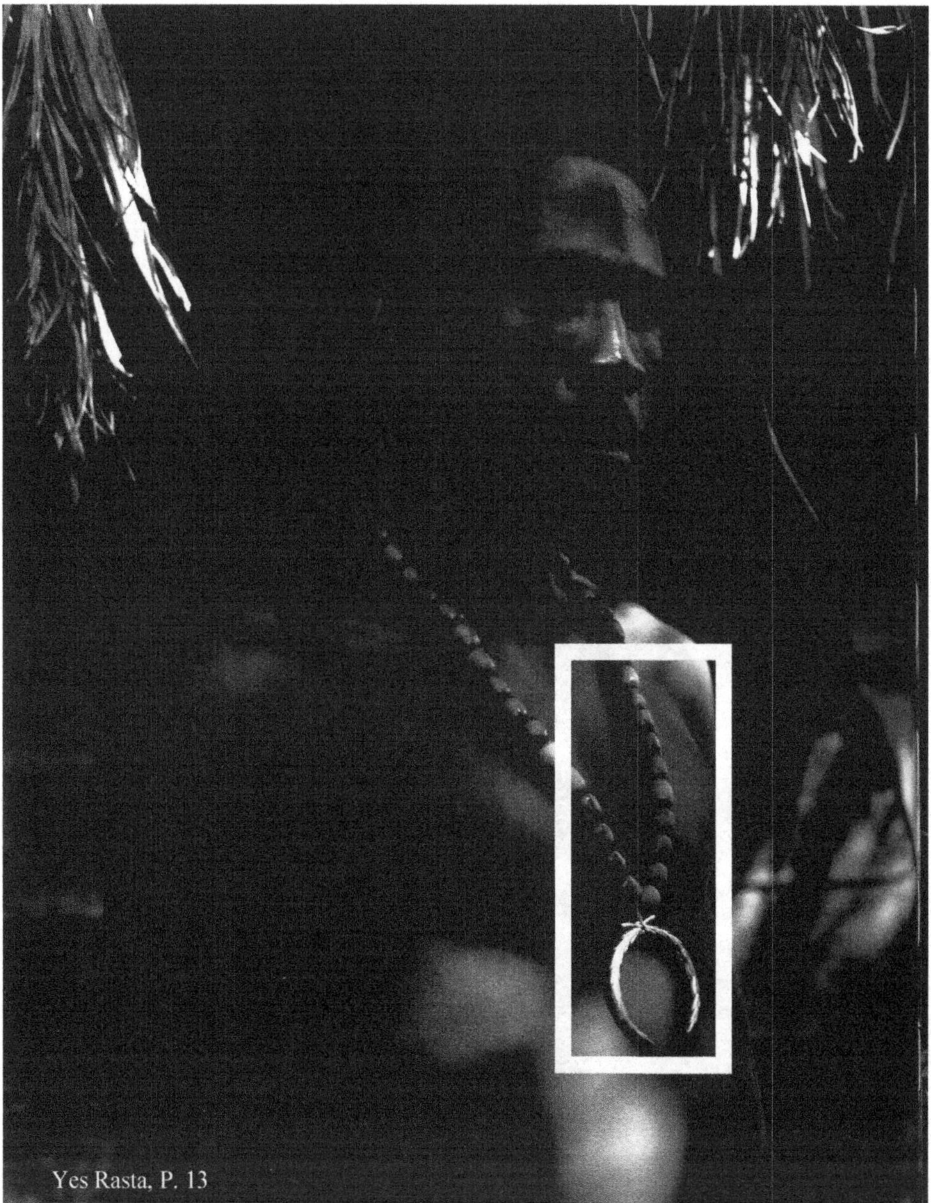
Yes Rasta, P. 13

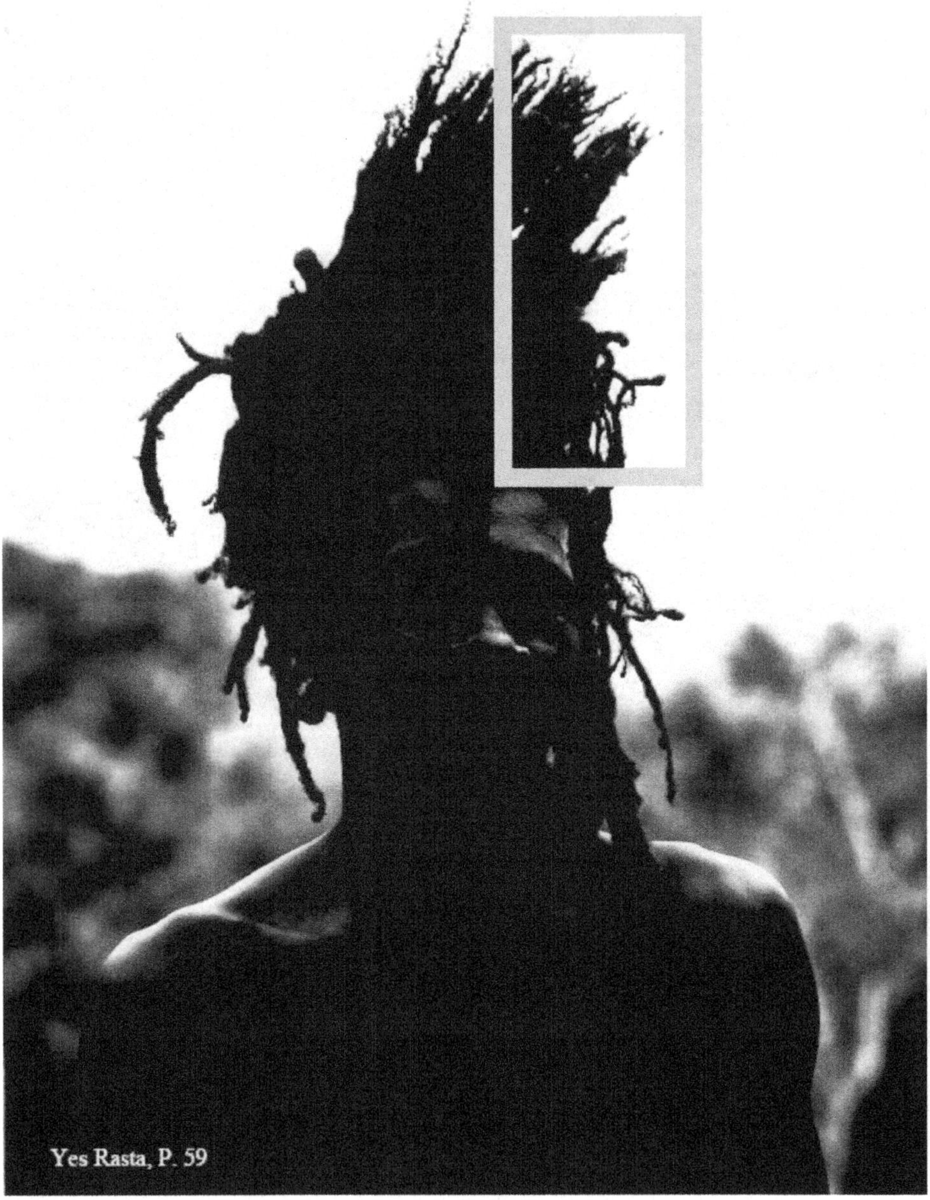

Yes Rasta, P. 59

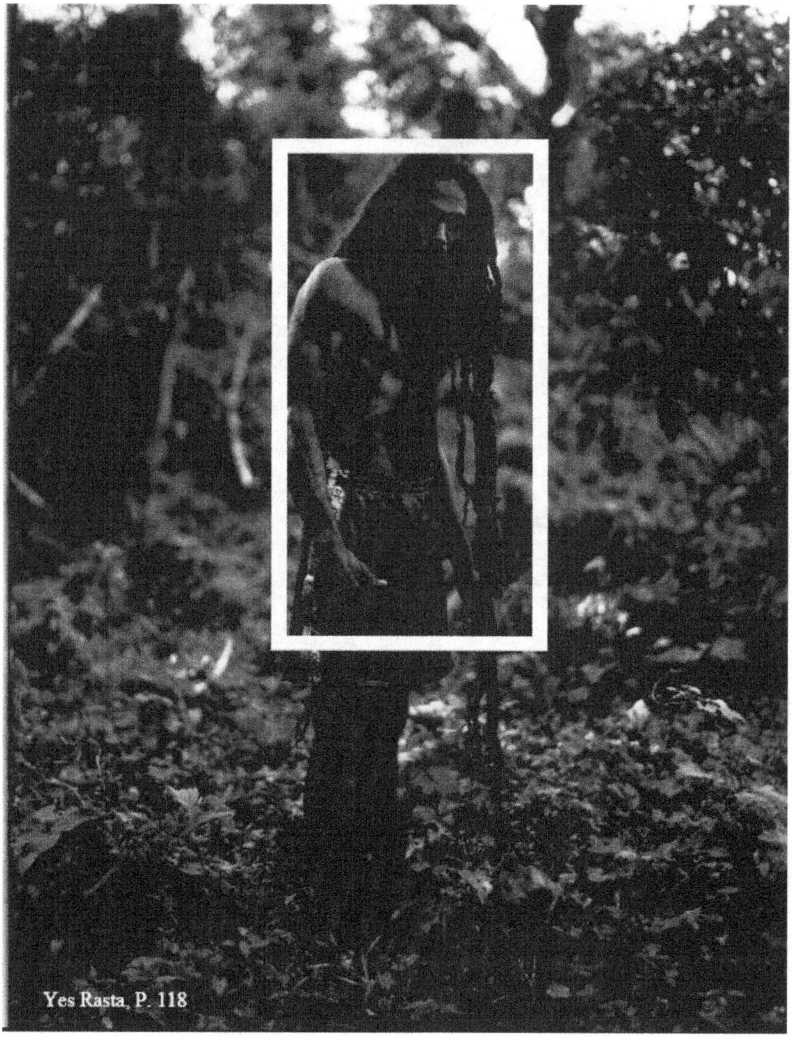
Yes Rasta, P. 118

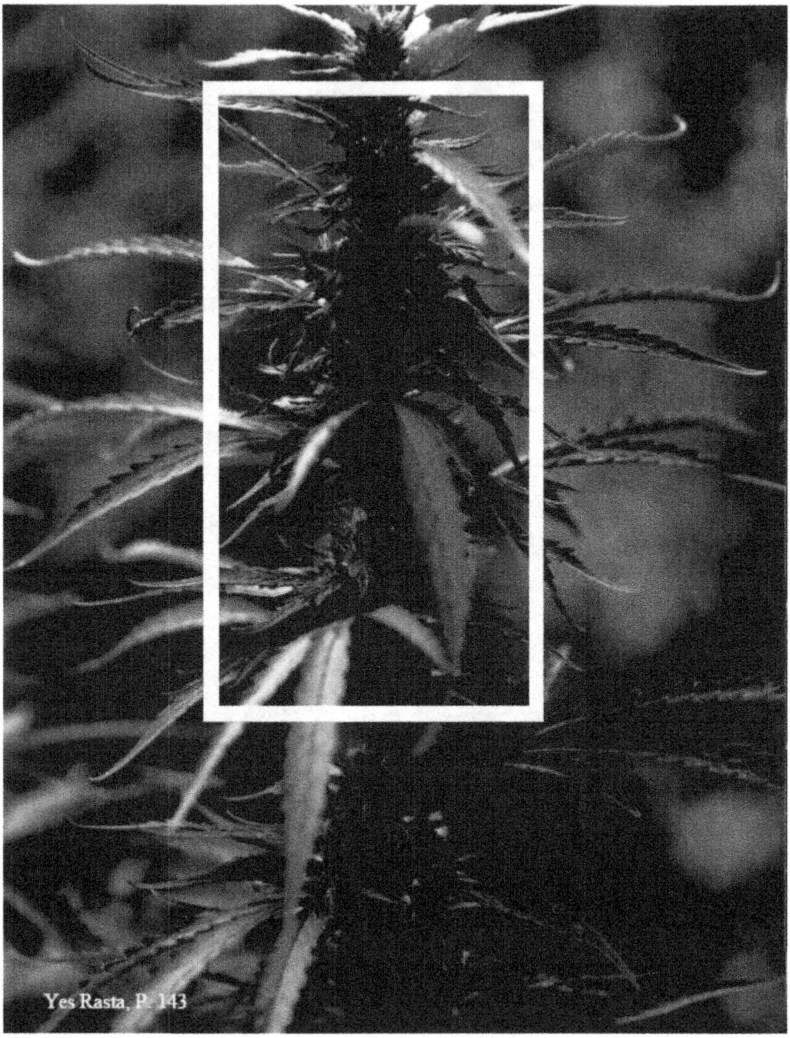
Yes Rasta, P. 143

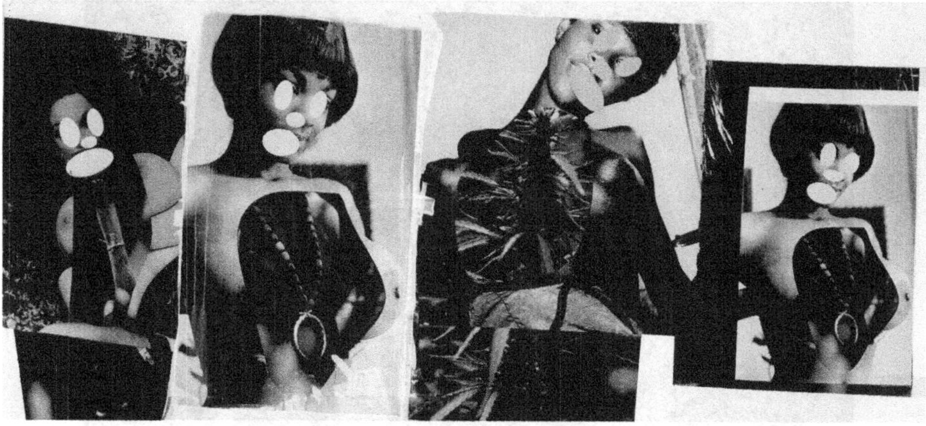

Z

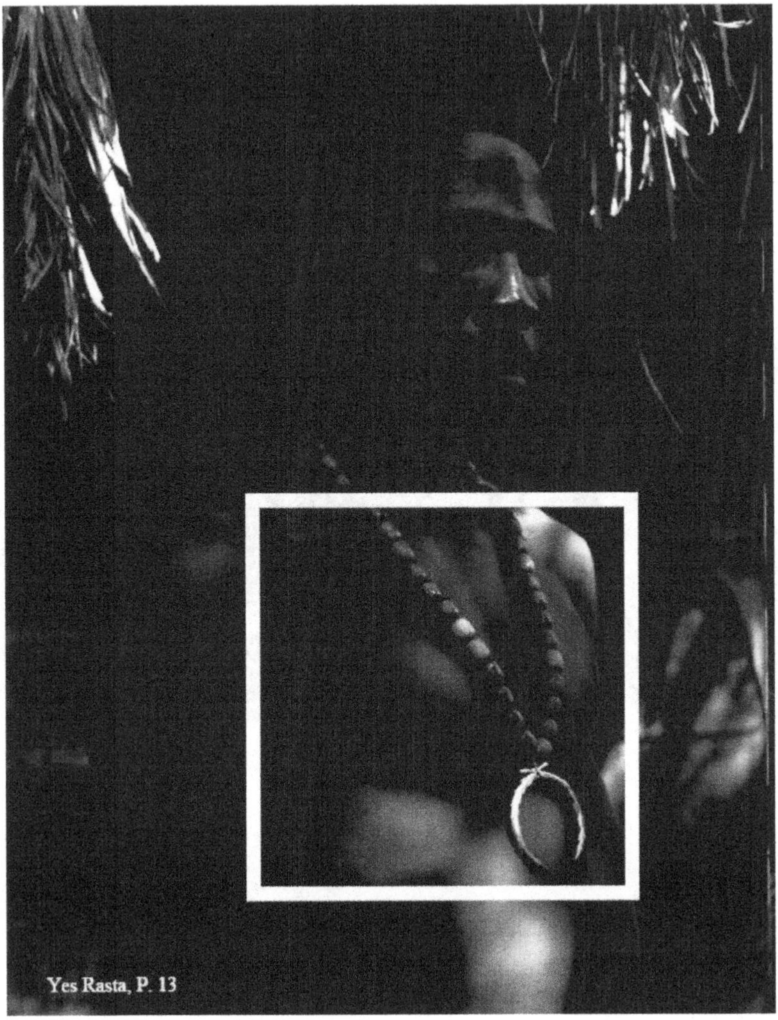

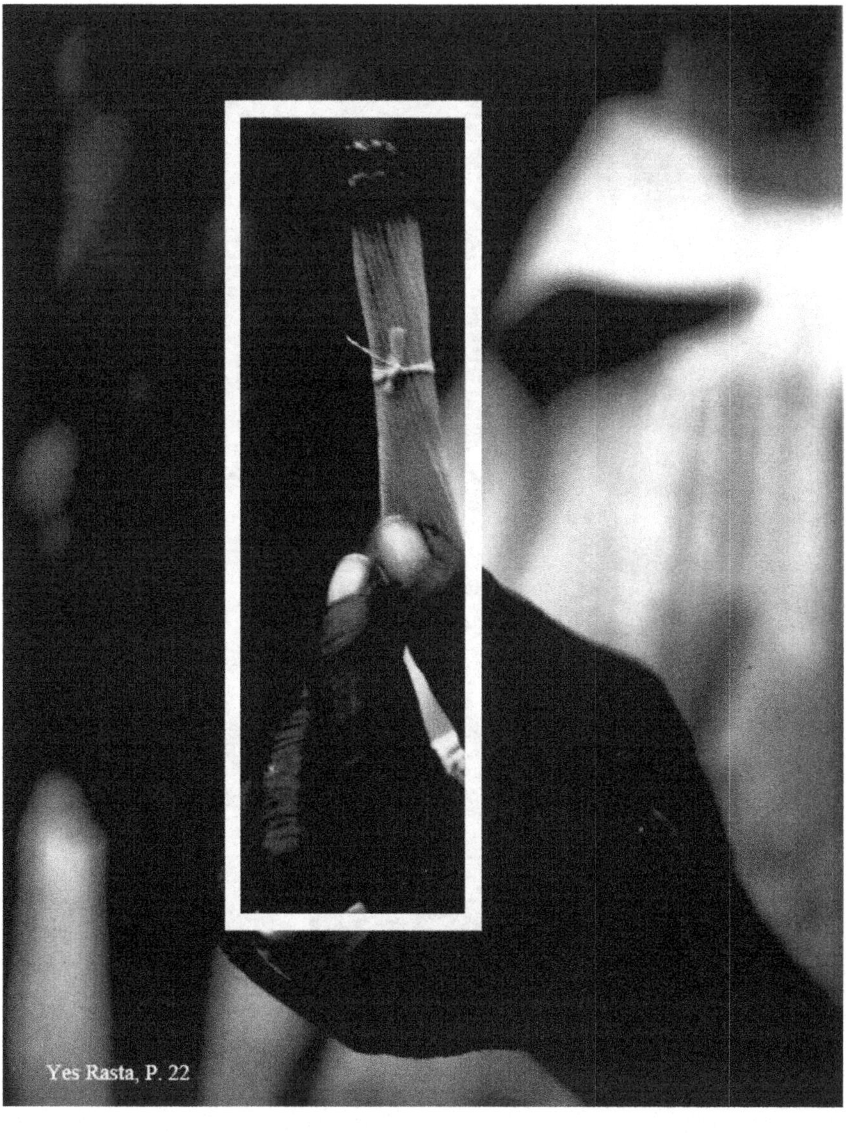
Yes Rasta, P. 22

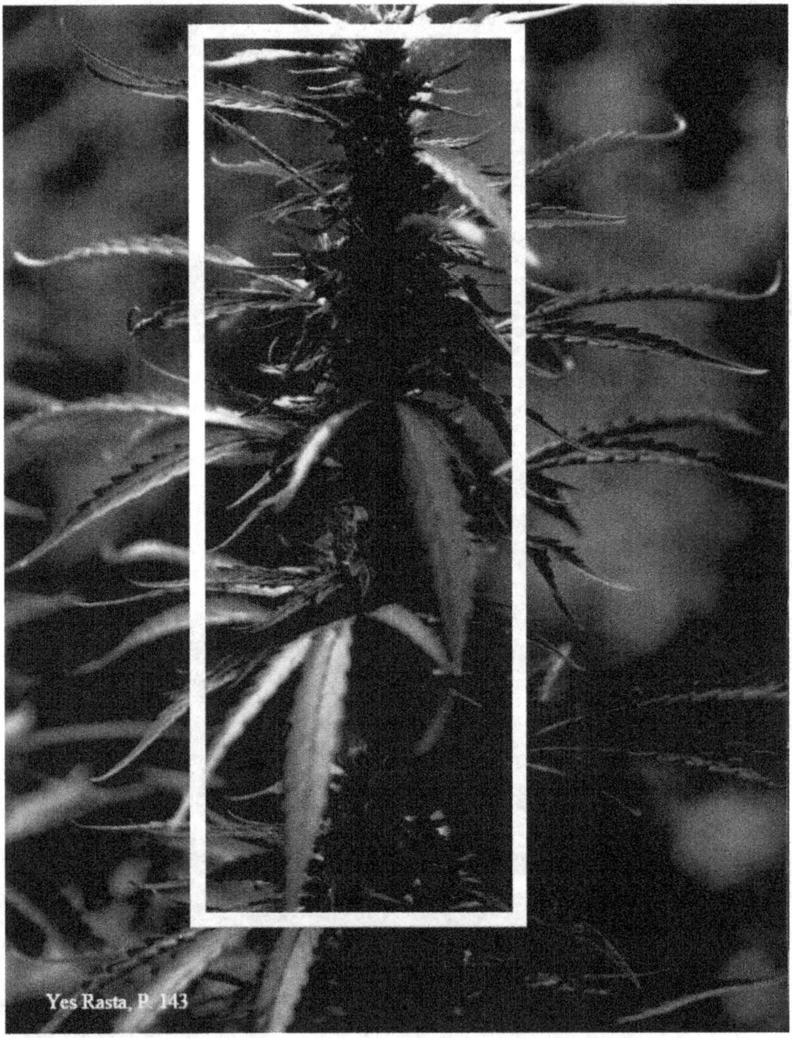
Yes Rasta, P. 143

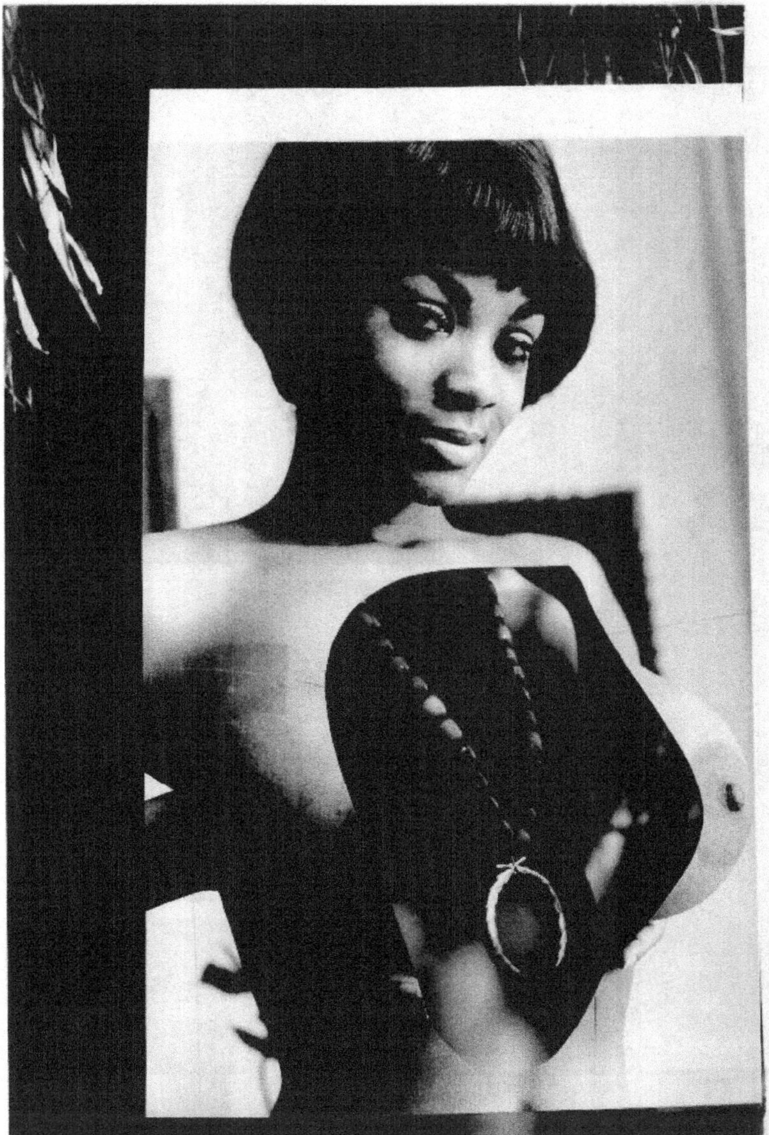

AA

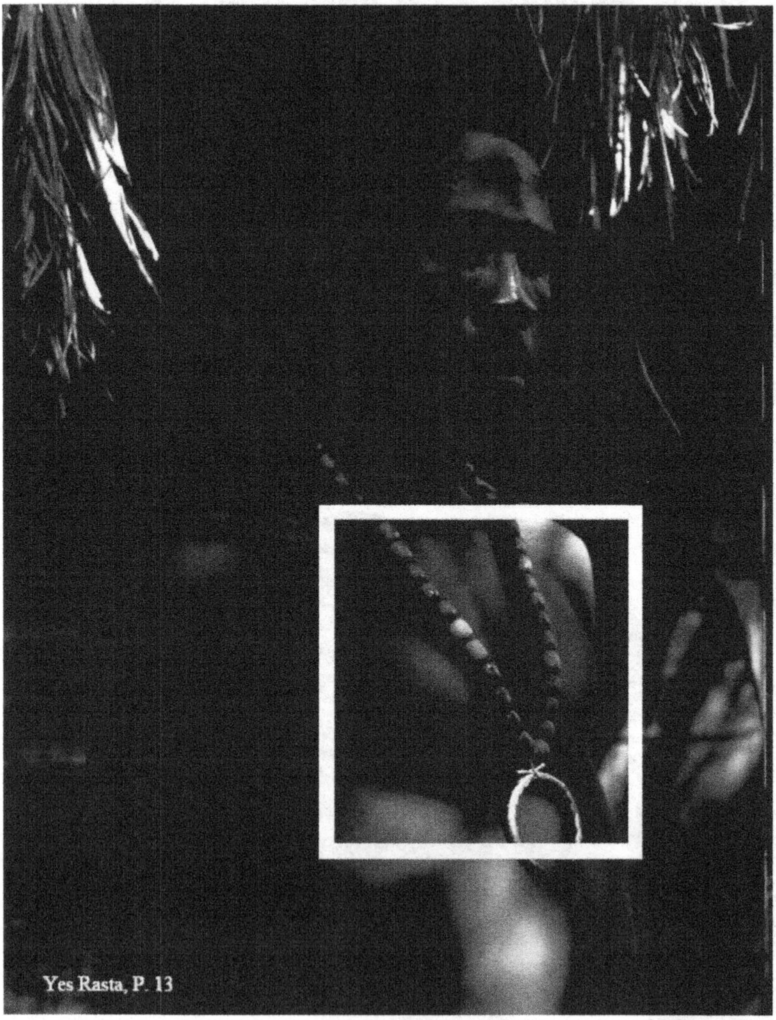

Yes Rasta, P. 13

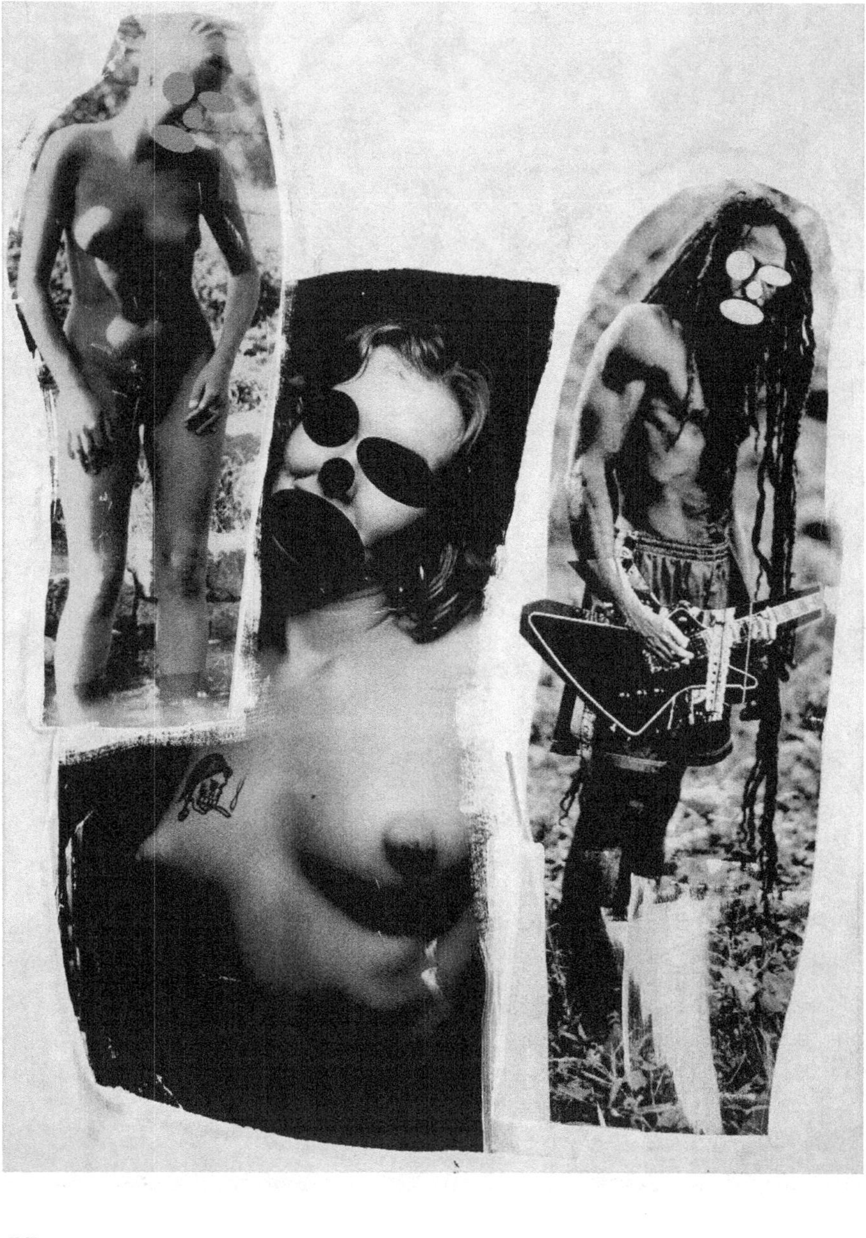

BB

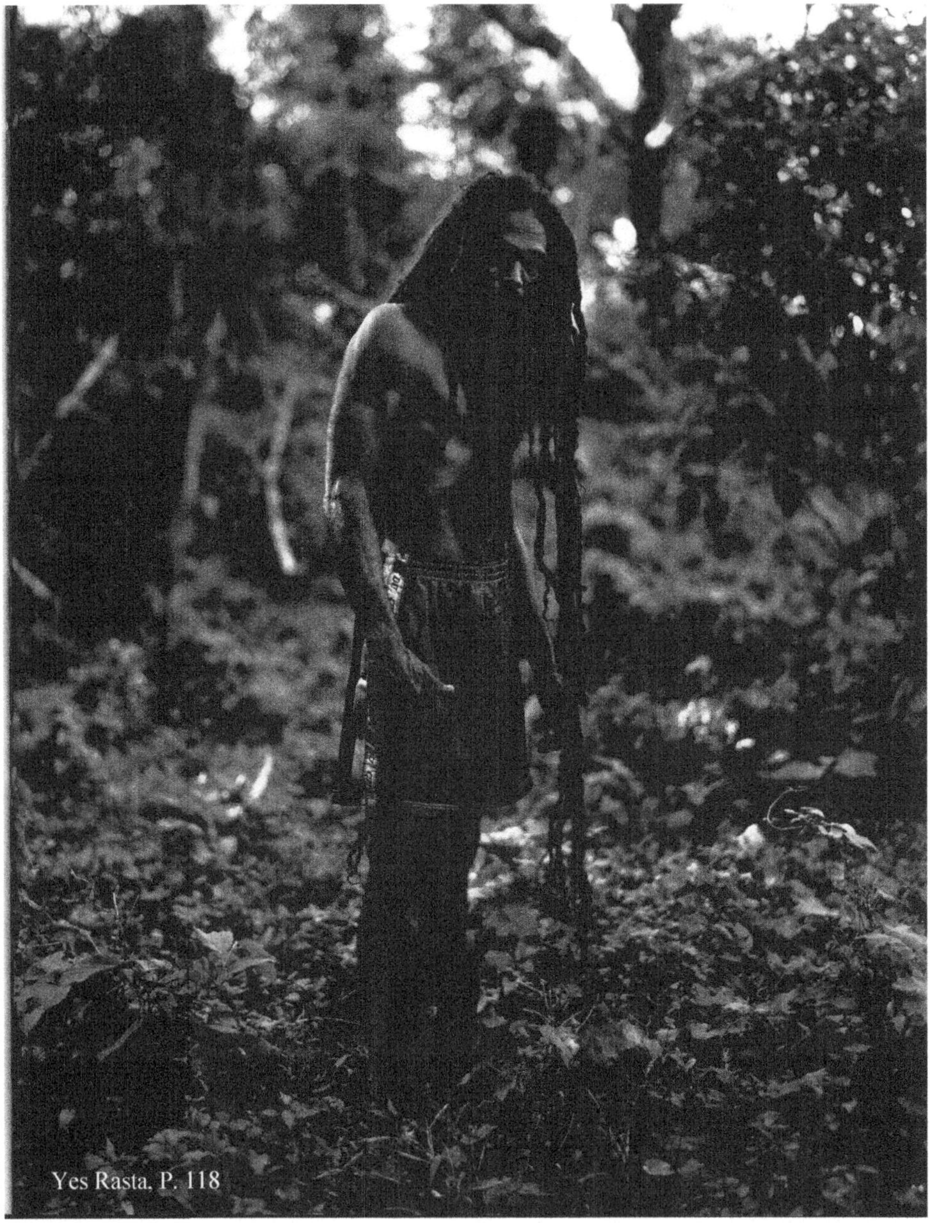
Yes Rasta, P. 118

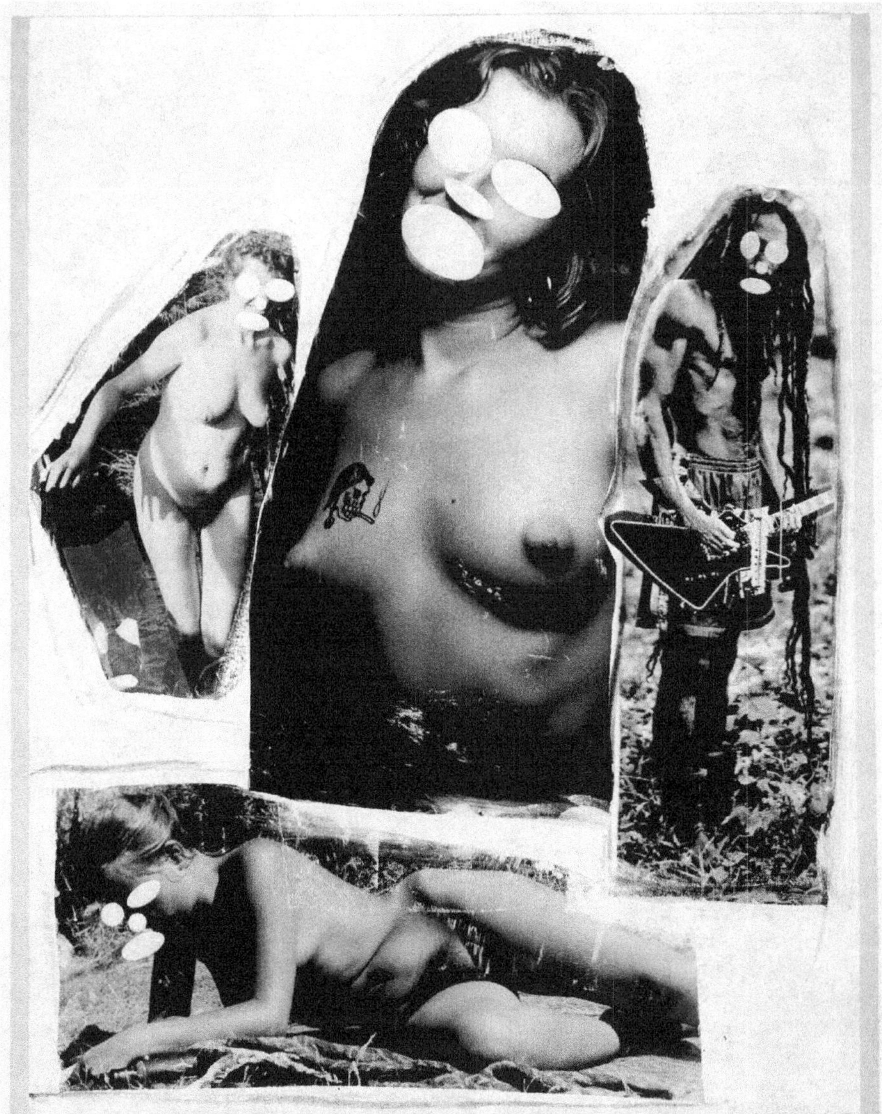

CC

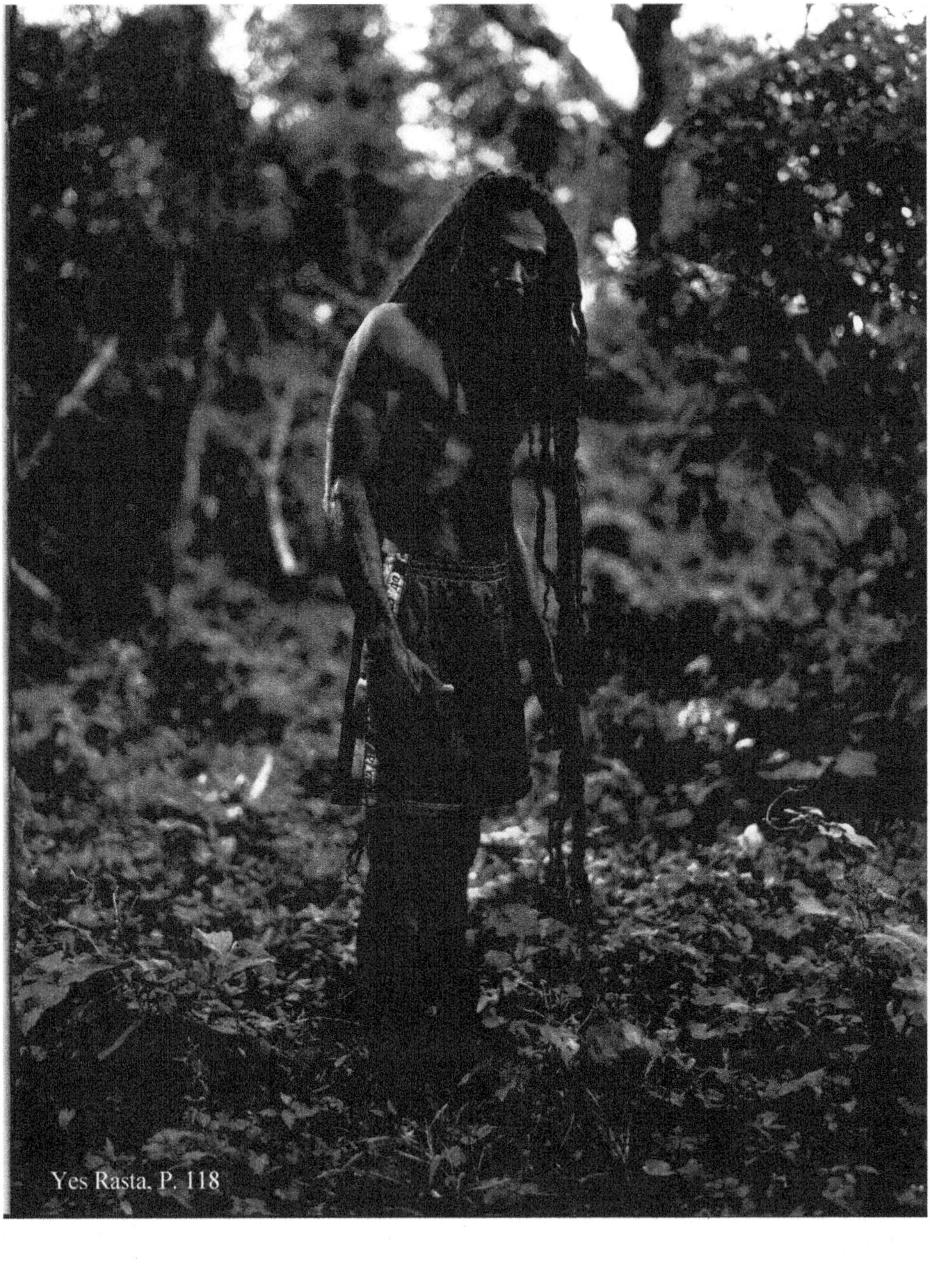

Yes Rasta. P. 118

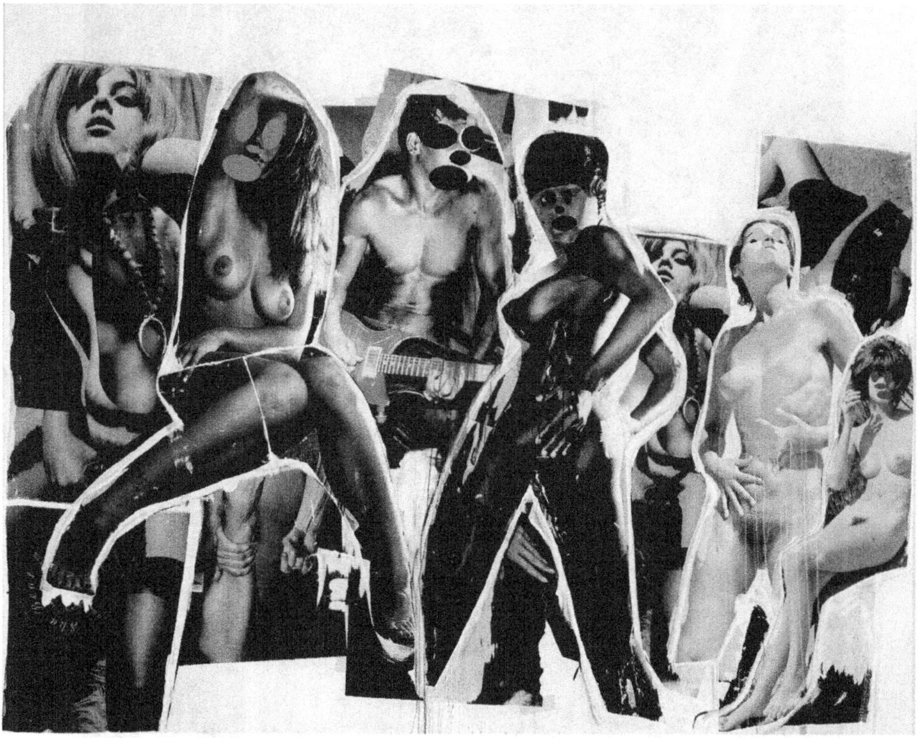

DD

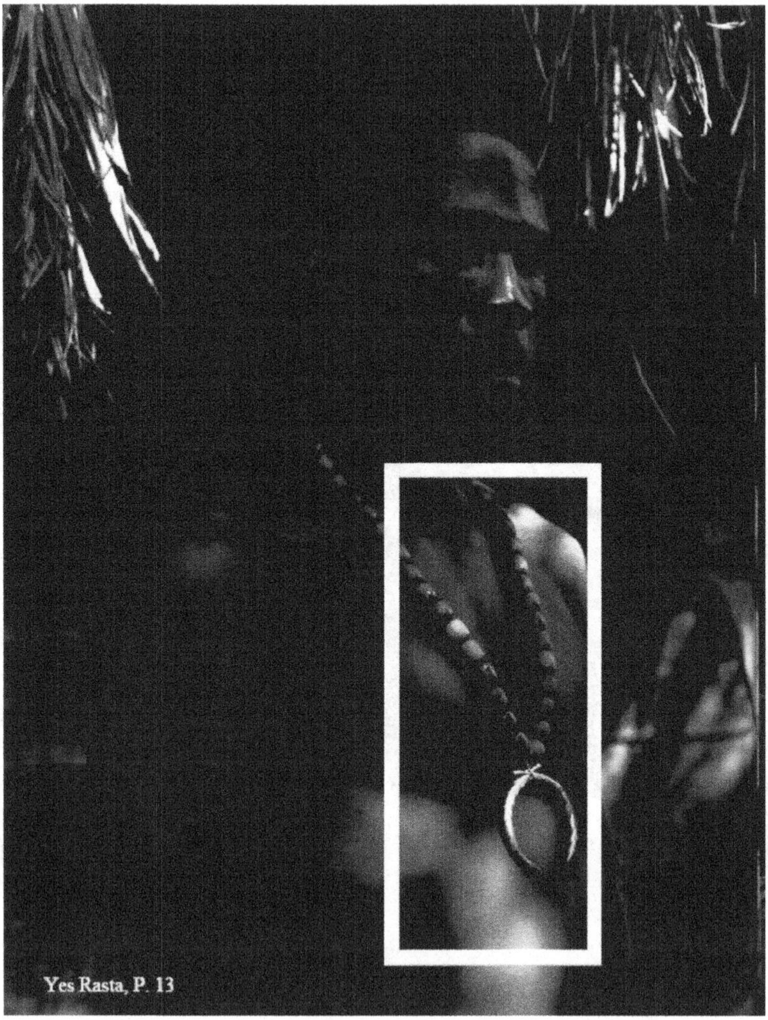
Yes Rasta, P. 13

Made in the USA
Monee, IL
04 November 2026

67385541R00079